Forward Edge of the Battle Area

Forward Edge of the Battle Area

A Chaplain's Story

Curt Bowers
as told to
Glen Van Dyne

Foreword by Brig. Gen. Dick Abel

Beacon Hill Press of Kansas City
Kansas City, Missouri

Copyright 1987
by Beacon Hill Press of Kansas City

Second Edition 1994

ISBN 083-411-2205

Printed in the
United States of America

Cover Design: Paul Franitza

10   9   8   7   6   5   4   3   2   1

CONTENTS

Foreword

Historians paint the Vietnam War with many different brushes. Some writers say it was justified. Others say it was unjustified and senseless. Only a few are ambivalent. The fact is that Vietnam was a war, not a conflict; one need only look at the numbers of men and women who gave their lives in service to their country. Military people don't argue about the rightness or wrongness but carry out our national policy.

Chaplains are part of that—as they serve to nurture and pastor the "flock" of the military within their command. Vietnam was a place that rattled not only buildings and equipment but also lives. Chaplains were there to attend to the business to which God had called them.

Chaplain Curt Bowers is one of those men—a man of great courage and resolve, and yet with a meekness of spirit and a care and concern for his flock. *Forward Edge of the Battle Area* takes you right to the front, where Chaplain Bowers served those in his command. He doesn't pull punches; he tells it as it was and shares how God used that opportunity to reach hundreds of men and women with Christ's love.

Take away Curt Bowers' chaplain's cross and his seminary training and put him in the field as an infantryman, and you'll find a spirit that is tough, a sinew that is strong, and a fiber that will stand with the best of them. But Curt Bowers was more. God took him and formed him into a useful vessel to serve Him in places normal pastors never go.

You will find this book to be heartrending and shocking. You will undoubtedly shed a tear. Your life will be changed because of the life of one chaplain whose only purpose was to serve God and to share His love with others.

—BRIG. GEN. DICK ABEL
Director, Military Ministry
Campus Crusade for Christ

Introduction

The war in Vietnam is history. Its battles have been fought and won or lost. But like all wars the impact will continue to be felt for decades to come.

For most people in the world it was a distant battlefield. Even though its scenes were transmitted daily into our living rooms by way of the five o'clock news, we felt a certain detachment from it. We fooled ourselves into thinking we could make it go away with a flick of the television button. We could not.

There were many battlefronts, not all in Southeast Asia. Some were on college campuses. Others intruded on the sanctity of our homes. Sharp differences of opinion divided us. We found that a nation divided against itself could not stand against the enemy. Like it or not, those of us who lived during those years found ourselves thrust into the fray.

Chaplain (Col.) Curt Bowers served in the war zone during the early years of conflict in Vietnam. His story is one of unashamed patriotism and loyalty as a soldier in the service of his country. Under orders by his commanding officer, he found himself on the forward edge of the battle. There, in obedience to a higher authority, the God who "makes wars cease to the ends of the earth" (Ps. 46:9, NIV), he faced life-and-death issues head-on.

No matter what your position regarding the war in Vietnam, you will find yourself facing life's serious issues as you read this chaplain's story. Battles are raging where you live and work. People are bleeding and dying as surely as they were in every war in history. The battles you and I face daily may be of greater consequence than even the great military confrontations. We too are called on to bring the presence of Jesus through our presence.

I am grateful for the privilege Chaplain Bowers has allowed me in being a part of the writing of this book. My respect for him as a person and for those he represents has grown much in the experience of helping get this story on paper. In the process I have come to a greater appreciation for all the brave and loyal men and women of the armed forces who have dared to stand at the battlefronts for us all.

The path of my journey through life has not taken me into the military service. As a pastor in Hawaii during the beginning years of United States involvement in Southeast Asia, I served a congregation in which the men and women of the 25th Infantry Division stationed at Schofield Barracks were a predominate part. It was there I gained some insights into the realities of being in uniform. While I did not serve on the forward edge of that or any other military battle, I stood by the families of those who marched into the face of the enemy, some never to return. I remember vividly the first official casualty of that war who was brought back to be buried in beautiful Punchbowl Cemetery in Honolulu, Captain Good. Somehow his name is a symbol to me of the good men and women who have answered the call to action in spiritual as well as physical battles.

As in battle, the support troops deserve more credit than they usually receive. Doris Bowers was there through virtually all the days her husband served in active duty in the military. She provided the insights and editing assistance that help bring warmth and feeling to this book. Mary Jo Van Dyne did the nitty-gritty work of entering the thoughts and words of the authors into the computer and then reentering all the changes again and again until the final manuscript was ready for the publisher's scrutiny.

Recently the leaders of a major denomination proposed taking the old hymn "Onward, Christian Soldiers" out of their official songbook. A grass-roots rebellion defeated the idea. It seems that Christians do understand they are engaged in a battle and that they must never beat a retreat. This book is offered with the prayer that Christians everywhere will find courage and strength as they follow the cross of Jesus into the forward edge of their battlefield.

—GLEN LEWIS VAN DYNE

1

Uncle Sam Wants You

It was a November day, but the long johns under my uniform kept me warm as I stood on the reviewing stand and watched the troops march by. Thoughts of beginning days in the army warmed my heart. Twenty-eight-year-old memories misted my eyes.

As deputy post chaplain I had been asked to speak at the commencement for a graduating class of basic trainees in Fort Knox, Ky. While presenting the awards and trooping the line, I remembered that day years before when I had stood where they were standing, as a volunteer for the draft in the Korean War.

Looking back, I remembered the emotional good-bye to my family in the Lancaster, Pa., Greyhound bus station. The Korean War was hot and heavy in October 1952. As I boarded the bus, I had no doubt that soon I would be on the battlefront somewhere on the 38th parallel.

When I joined the army, I was not a professing Christian. After graduating from high school at age 17 and working for 2 years, I found myself still searching desperately for meaning and direction. Maybe that's why I enlisted—I wasn't content with my lot in life. There was the feeling that maybe I could find God somewhere by leaving home. The recent death of my Boy Scout leader at a very young age had given me my first encounter with death. Riding the bus toward Fort Knox, I began to think about what would happen if I suddenly died without Christ.

Soon heavy feelings of loneliness, danger, and separation from the family overcame me. It did not take long for the shock of suddenly being in the military service to leave its mark. All around were people attempting to satisfy their desires with sex, drugs, and alcohol. Without the freedom and comforts of civilian life to enjoy, I soon learned the value of phone calls and letters. They were a vital part of my survival kit.

Entering basic training with the Korean War in mind made for more serious thoughts about God. While taking bayonet training, I listened to the war stories of sergeants and officers who had recently returned from Korea. I knew that if my lot was to be an infantryman, I had a good chance of being brought back in a body bag from Korea. I loved our home, our relatives, and our friends in the Pennsylvania Dutch country and wanted someday to return.

But God had plans for me other than Korea. Because of some mechanical ability I had acquired in high school, the army assigned me to a tank outfit in Germany.

The shipboard trip to Germany was long and boring for soldiers jammed into cramped quarters. There was not much to do but sit on the cold deck and watch the water of the North Atlantic splash against the bow of the ship. One day Bob Kilheffer and I (we had been good friends since civilian days in Lancaster) conspired to have an impromptu Fourth of July celebration to spice things up a bit. I had brought along some firecrackers in my duffle bag. We threw a

14

couple of them, not thinking about the intense danger of fire aboard ship. You can guess the rest of the story. The ship's captain took a very dim view of the situation and summoned the military police to bring us into custody. My reward for livening up the day was an immediate order to serve in the kitchen police force the rest of the voyage.

Upon debarking, I found myself assigned to duty in Bamberg, Germany. There God brought me into contact with a chaplain. From the beginning of military service, I had felt it was my duty to go to church. In basic training I went because of a fear of the unknown. Now, looking forward to a year of living in Germany, I was tempted to let this habit drift and forget about chapel. But thanks to my parents instilling the habit during growing-up years, I continued out of tradition.

Now I wasn't particularly attracted to the chaplain's message. Square-jawed, with piercing blue eyes and hair parted up the middle, this Dutchman from New York State preached a gospel I had never heard before. I went and listened but was miserable. Other soldiers went forward to the altar to pray and accept Jesus as their Savior and Lord. I wanted Him desperately, too, but was not willing to pay the price. I tried to convince myself that I was a Christian. Hadn't I been dedicated and confirmed and joined the church? So I kept pushing the conviction off on the others who were engaged in outward sins and things I was trying to avoid. But all the time I knew I was a phony.

The chaplain's wife didn't help a bit. She would invite us over to their home after the evening service for coffee and cake, and all the time she would talk about having a "know-so" salvation.

Then Chaplain Van Vorce told the story of how

his son was converted in a spiritual awakening at Asbury College. It was the revival that swept that campus in the early 1950s and spread across the country to other Christian college campuses. His son felt a call to the ministry and set out to prepare. Then in a tragic construction accident he was electrocuted. It was shortly after this funeral service for his son that Chaplain Van Vorce was sent to Germany.

As I attended those chapel services and watched many from our battalion and other battalions come to the Lord, the conviction mounted. The chaplain and his wife would sing with tears cascading down their cheeks. I felt the power of God in a way I never had in my life. There was an overwhelming sense of the peace and presence of God. I found myself drawn to hear the chaplain speak in service after service.

One evening he invited us to close the evening service in prayer around the altar. As I was kneeling there that night, he asked for anybody who needed special prayer to raise his hand. Feeling that I needed to know Jesus, I raised my hand. As he laid his hand on me to pray, I felt the touch of heaven on my shoulder and asked him to help me pray the prayer of repentance. Christ did indeed come into my heart. It was a beautiful experience. For the first time in my young adult life I could now say that Jesus had forgiven all my sins and that I was a Christian!

2

Someone Else Wants You

My assignment as a tank mechanic often brought out the worst in me. One uncomfortably hot day while I was contorted over a tank engine, the wrench broke loose from a nut I was trying to loosen. My knuckles spurted blood. The sudden pain was unbearable. Impulsively, I picked up the closest thing handy, a flashlight, and threw it against the shop wall, shattering it to pieces. The language I used to express my feelings in that moment was not a good verbal witness to my newfound faith in Christ. My roommate, Bronco, was nearby and heard my outburst. I had been trying to convince him to go to church with me.

"Curt, I thought you were a Christian," he said. "You certainly don't sound like one."

Anger and resentment surged within me. What right did Bronco have to judge me? But when I cooled down a bit, I knew in my heart he was right. The longer I thought about it, the more remorseful I became. What's gone wrong here? I thought. There must be more to being a Christian than this. As soon as I could, I was off to see the chaplain again.

Chaplain Van Vorce assured me that God still loved me—just as I was—and had not forsaken me. Patiently he explained that I was trying to live the Christian life by my own strength rather than by the power of the presence of Christ within me. He helped me understand that I was rebelling against God's authority in my life. I realized he was right. There was a good deal of pride and selfishness still lurking inside me, leading me to do things my way instead of God's way. Together we searched the Scriptures. We read passages like 1 Thess. 3:10, in which Paul spoke to early Christians about something "lacking" in their faith. He pointed out 1 Cor. 3:16 and 6:19, which teach that our bodies are to be the temple of God, where the Spirit of God dwells in us.

We talked long into the night. My strong self-will raised all the arguments it could muster against the idea that I must surrender the lordship of my life to Jesus completely and allow Him to be my "Supreme Commander."

From childhood I had believed I should do everything I could to be "king of the block" and take care of things in my own way. This self-reliant attitude had now turned on me and stood in the way of letting Jesus be Lord as well as Savior. In my heart I knew that God could do much better with my life than I was doing. But I was afraid to turn loose. I trusted God to rule the universe but wanted Him to keep His fingers out of my affairs.

Finally around midnight I prayed another prayer. This time I asked Jesus not only to live inside me but to be on the throne of my innermost being.

Another soldier, Bill Rebman, had gone with me that night to visit the chaplain. He too was seeking answers for similar needs in his life. Bill was quicker to catch on than I and more emotional in his response. As we left the chaplain's fourth-floor apartment, he was exuberant.

"I feel like dancing on a cloud!" he exclaimed.

"The sky has never been so beautiful! The stars never looked so good!"

But I didn't feel that way at all. There was no "out of this world" feeling for me. As we walked home, old doubts arose, and I felt rather depressed. But then I decided just to let it rest, believing I had done all I knew to do. If God wanted me to feel or act any differently, it was going to be up to him, since I had prayed for Him to be Lord of everything I was or ever hoped to be.

As I was brushing my teeth before retiring for the night, I looked into the mirror and suddenly felt an overwhelming sense of God's presence. He revealed himself to me in an almost audible voice.

"Curt, you have done all you can do. Trust Me to work in you and give you the peace and power you need."

That night I slept more soundly than I had in many years. The real test would come in the morning.

For a long time I had carried on a continuous battle with a Corporal Farley. He seemed to be doing everything he could to keep me confined to quarters, which prevented me from seeing a special girl I had come to know in Germany. His weekly objective was to see that I was in attendance at a "GI party" every Friday night (mopping and cleaning the area to get everything spic and span for inspection). He took great delight in knowing that Friday was the only night to see my girl. I had hated him for it.

I had retaliated with regularity. I was in charge of physical training for our company of men, so I had taken that opportunity to run him into the ground. I liked to see him sweat and moan. This had gone on and on, each of us after the other in passive-aggressive ways (usually more aggressive than passive).

So the next morning when I encountered Corporal Farley and he threw a mop at me, I knew the experience of the night before was more than an emotional high. The usual resentment and animosity toward him were gone. I didn't hate him anymore. Instead, I saw him as one for whom I should pray and share what God had done for me.

The poem "When I Met the Master" (author unknown) sums up what had begun to happen inside me.

> I had walked life's path with an easy tread,
> Had followed where comfort and pleasure led;
> And then one day in a quiet place
> I met the Master, face to face.
>
> With station and rank and wealth for a goal,
> Much thought for the body but none for the soul,
> I had thought to win in life's mad race,
> When I met the Master, face to face.
>
> I had built my castles and reared them high,
> Till their towers pierced the blue of the sky;
> I had vowed to rule with an iron mace,
> When I met the Master, face to face.
>
> I met Him and knew Him, and blushed to see
> That eyes full of sorrow were turned on me;
> And I faltered and fell at His feet that day,
> While all my castles melted and vanished away—
>
> Melted and vanished and in their place,
> I saw naught else but my Master's face;
> And I cried aloud: "Oh, make me meet
> To follow the path of Thy wounded feet."

And now thoughts are for the souls of men;
I've lost my life, to find it again.
E'er since that day in a quiet place
*I met the Master, face to face.**

Love really does find a way. God's love showed me a way to deal with my hate and anger and all the other negative things inside me that were tearing me down. Human love finds a way too. In spite of the obstacles, I found ways to get off the post to see this special girl, Doris Shawver. Her dad, incidentally, was the post engineer of the Bamberg Kaserne. After getting things settled spiritually in my life, this relationship took on added meaning.

*From *Beautiful Poems on Jesus,* comp. Basil Miller (Kansas City: Beacon Hill Press, 1948), 203-4.

PFC Curt Bowers and Doris in a Bamberg,
Germany, park, 1953.

Before leaving Germany, I took a train to Grindel-wald, Switzerland, and then on into Cortina, Italy. I went skiing in the Alps. It was a very special time of feeling exceptionally close to God. Reading the Bible and a book on the subject of knowing the will of God turned my mind to just what God was calling me to—a life of full-time service in the ministry. As much as I knew my own heart, I let go of every selfish ambition and desire to be my own man and do my own thing and said, "Yes, Lord, one eternal yes. I'll do what You want me to do."

And so my call to the ministry was settled. For the first time in my life there was a sense of harmony and peace about why I was in this world.

I shared with Doris the growing feeling I had that God might be calling me to go to college. Until this time, college had been the farthest thing from my mind. Now I wanted to go to a Christian college, to prepare for whatever God was calling me to do. Doris was already planning to attend Duke University. Rather selfishly I prayed the Lord would change her mind, and she would want to go where I was going to go.

That prayer was answered, and Doris joined me and six other young men, all of whom had been called to the ministry under Chaplain Van Vorce's ministry, in entering Asbury College at the same time. The years would separate most of us as we went all over the world as missionaries and ministers. I determined that Doris would be the one exception to this matter of saying good-by to my army buddies and college friends.

While at Asbury, I spent four years as a student pastor. During that time I was approved by my de-nomination as a staff specialist (second lieutenant) in the army in preparation for ministry. It seemed that God was leading me into the chaplaincy. My life had come full circle, since it was there I had found a vital, life-changing faith in Christ. I felt I could serve Him and share my faith with many young men and women who were going through the same things I had experienced earlier in the military service of my country.

In 1960 I became an ordained elder in my chosen denomination—nothing short of a miracle! The church officials also gave me their endorsement for the chaplaincy, should that ever open up.

After traveling to Washington, D.C., to check on the possibility of becoming an army chaplain, I was shocked and disappointed. I was candidly told that the quota for my denomination was already exceeded, and that it would be seven years before there would be an opening for a chaplain. Greatly disappointed, I went back home believing Heb. 11:1, that "faith is the assurance of the things we hope for, the proof of the reality of the things we cannot see" (Williams).

That beautiful girl I had managed to date despite the corporal's best-laid plans became my wife. Through an anxious time of preparation, she was my greatest human support. I threw myself into the work and responsibility of pastoring a small home mission church in New Jersey, but the vision to be a military chaplain burned deep in my soul. Only Doris, who knew me thoroughly and understood the great need for committed chaplains in the military, kept my hopes high. We planned to minister seven years so that we could be where we felt God's call the strongest—in the chaplaincy.

Wonder of wonders! Before we had served a year

in that church, I received a phone call from Washington, D.C., with the message: "If you're still interested in active duty, we will send you. Your assignment is classified secret, so come to Washington. I can't tell you over the phone where you're going."

That's how I found myself in Fort Huachuca, Ariz., for my first assignment as an army chaplain. The entire Signal Battalion had been getting ready to deploy to Germany. Chaplain Morton, the man in charge of assignments, had been thinking about someone to fill the battalion chaplain's billet. Some army area signal centers were being set up as a new concept in battlefield communications strategy. The Holy Spirit brought my name to his mind, and he called me immediately. Needless to say, we were ecstatic and thankful that God had opened the door for this assignment.

Much as we loved our congregation and hated to leave them, the call to serve the church in the military was overwhelming. So back to Germany we went, our hearts thrilled with the prospect of what lay ahead.

3

The Chaplain as Pastor

From the beginning, as a chaplain in the army, I considered it a privilege to minister to the men and women of the United States military services. Serving with them in a constantly changing and dangerous world, I could offer them hope and faith in an unchanging and caring God as seen in Jesus Christ. We were in Germany at a time when service personnel were called on to keep the peace. We were charged with carrying out our national mission of peace through strength.

Many people who join the service regret it as a kind of "time-out" of their lives. How far from the truth such an attitude is! I wanted to make this experience a constructive one and to give them the opportunity to know the risen Lord. Military service offers the chaplain many opportunities for personal evangelism. Many under his spiritual care are in the throes of considering some of the greatest questions of life:

"Who am I and how can I learn to relate to others?"

"What will occupy the working years of my life?"

"How do I relate to the opposite sex?"

"Whom should I marry?"

"What do I believe?"

Preaching, teaching, and conducting worship services were the major tasks during those three years in Germany. Conducting morning services in the chapel, which had not had a full-time schedule of services for years, was a challenge. Later on we developed an evening fellowship and worship, as well as a Wednesday-night Bible study.

I was proud to be a part of the chaplaincy—a service that goes back farther than our own nation's history. Opportunities to witness for Christ in the military seemed unlimited.

There is something exciting about preaching the Word of God to a congregation made up of people from a variety of backgrounds. In a typical chapel service a wide spectrum of Protestantism is represented.

While overseas assignments sound romantic to those who have never been on them, nevertheless there can be much loneliness and boredom that serve as hindrances to Christian living. I discovered two advantages to the chaplaincy, perhaps greater than the civilian ministry—access and visibility. A chaplain must live and work with his people. He goes to the same gym, commissary, post exchange; wears the same uniform; and is a part of the commander's staff. As an integral part of the team, he is welcome in any part of the office, shop, flight line, aircraft, or ship. He serves on boards and committees that are involved in the welfare of the military community. The insignia he wears, the chaplain's cross, is symbolic of his ongoing ministry at every moment.

As a chaplain I was often chided by civilian ministers who would say to me, "When are you coming back into the ministry?" It seemed difficult for them to understand that we had never gone away from our ministry. In fact, we were in it up to our ears. We were heavily involved in trying to bring others to Christ—evangelizing the unsaved, as well as shepherding—pastoring the sheep. We were active participants in the life of the military community. We asked God to bless banquets, sporting events, graduations, and facilities. Where people were, we were there to minister. Every day we counseled with men and women who otherwise might never have darkened the door of a church as we assisted people in solving their problems.

Chaplains are expected to conduct memorial services, funerals, baptisms, marriages, and Communion services. How could one have a more pastoral ministry? Chaplains teach Bible study and doctrinal studies, along with classes in church membership, teacher training, family life, and marriage. They are pastors—pastors in uniform who continue to visit the sick and the bereaved. So if some cannot think of them as pastors in the military, they should try thinking about

Easter Sunrise Service, Camp Zama, Japan, 1972.
Chaplain Bowers on the right.

them as missionaries in the military. They really have not left the ministry. They have left the safety of their homes (their bunkers) and have gone to the forward edge of the battle for men's souls.

Since so many of the military are married, a chaplain ministers to the entire family. There are some circumstances that make for even greater stress in a military situation, such as isolation from the extended family, long distances from home, a culture foreign to one's background, and financial problems. All these things make the availability of a spiritual, pastoral person more critical.

One chaplain related the story of how he had to go tell a young wife that she had become a widow that morning. As he gently broke the news of her husband's death, she became hysterical—screaming, crying, moaning. Nothing anyone could do would calm her. Finally she had to be taken to the hospital. The chaplain learned later that she and her husband had fought that morning. She hadn't wanted him to leave to fly practice missions and had shouted to him, "I hope you don't come back!" Dealing with stress is part of a chaplain's ministry.

Many Americans in the military who are sent overseas take with them a sort of ghetto mentality. In the unfamiliar environment of a strange country, they can develop the feeling of being second-class citizens. That is why the chapel becomes a place of togetherness in ways more dramatic than in their home country or state. There is a closeness that develops across denominational lines. Trust in the Lord sustains us all regardless of our church backgrounds.

It is a great thing to be able to represent God to servicemembers. The disadvantages of serving in the military are often blown all out of proportion. The military complex in the United States is well organized and in most areas very efficient. A typical installation has an elaborate support system for dependents. It has a full-fledged school system, extensive recreational facilities, and a vast network of clubs, organizations, and activities. The leadership believes that a happy soldier is a good soldier, and that he won't be happy if he is missing his wife and children. When he has an overseas assignment, the family joins him where it is possible.

My wife's background was that of a "military brat." She was used to moving all over the country. Now I know that people who live in one place all their lives have their roots down deep, and that is an advantage, but they still miss a lot. For Doris and me, military life was very rewarding. Of course I believe that she was called to the chaplaincy as much as I was. She had a healthy, strong view of family and was very flexible and adaptive. We also believe our children are better prepared for this mobile society because they have moved often.

There is a disadvantage to such a lifestyle. It is difficult to get very close to people because it doesn't take them long to move on. Doris and I found we needed each other even more overseas and had much to contribute to each other's lives. Of course the hardest part of pastoring military people is departure—leaving friends, family, and assignments.

The greatest expectation placed upon a chaplain's wife is to be a real person. Doris made the most of the opportunity—playing the piano, singing in the choir, helping with the programs, and counseling other wives. She found herself involved in Bible study groups with women from all denominations.

Those days in Germany for us were tremendous

days of beginning. While they created quite a few demands on us in our first assignment, we learned with joy to walk confidently and boldly into a ministry that allowed us contact with people from many different backgrounds. It was good to be in the service of our country, representing the Highest Authority.

My experience as a chaplain in the military was teaching me to appreciate much about other denominations. I liked the navy slogan "Cooperation without compromise." Another quote often made, "In essentials, unity; in nonessentials, liberty; in all things, charity," took on a new meaning for me in the military. I discovered that there was room to worship according to one's own convictions even in a pluralistic world.

While the military is definitely not a religious organization, the conscience of its leadership recognizes that it deprives men and women of the traditional right to worship. Therefore the military in the United States has accepted the responsibility of providing spiritual leadership through its chaplaincy. If the church had to pay for chaplains to minister in the military, it would be an enormous expense. Then, when you remember that the military also provides housing and schools for chaplains' children, it is obvious we simply could not afford it. Thank God for a nation that allows this kind of spiritual ministry to people otherwise neglected!

As I carried on a ministry in Germany, I determined to go out into the field with the troops whenever possible. In the damp, cold weather I spent time with the men in the muddy fields, in their tanks and jeeps, sleeping wherever a place could be found, and as often as possible, holding services for them. This meant sometimes traveling 150 miles in a circuit in an

Chaplain's assistant setting up for a
field service, using the hood of my jeep, dubbed
Circuit Rider by the troops.

open jeep in the cold of winter in order to hold three
or four services with the signal units scattered all over
Germany. Had I chosen simply to stay close to the
chapel area, the average soldier would never have
seen me. The only contact with many of the men was
in the field. So with dust in my teeth or mud caked on
my boots, I was able to tell them about Christ. My
ministry became a matter of presence. Just being there
was a large part of it.

I will never forget some of my conversations with
the enlisted men and officers in the field. We had good
rap sessions especially at night, when they were off duty and not much was going on. I became friends with
some of our young officers and a crusty old warrant officer, Mr. Polk who had served in World War II. I listened to many of his war stories with rapt attention.
We became good friends, and he started coming to
chapel. When he was away from his tent one evening, I

31

put Limburger cheese on his potbellied stove. It really stank up the entire sleeping quarters. Needless to say, retribution was swift the next night. My assistant and I found our tent on top of us after all the tent pegs were pulled. It's a wonder he still talked to me. However, we did enjoy one another's company. Though I never had the privilege to personally lead him to Christ, some years later I heard he had become a Christian. I rejoiced in the privilege of sowing and cultivating the soil in order that somebody else could reap.

In the same way, navy chaplains have found that in the narrow passages below deck, a sailor will stop them and begin with, "Chaplain, there is something I have been meaning to ask you." Talking to the chaplain about his family problems and the problems of being separated from his loved ones is a great therapy for the lonely sailor. You see, Christ was crucified on the Cross, rose from the grave, and lives in human life where people swear and sweat, laugh and weep, win and lose, live and die. That's what Christ was about and still is.

That is what the chaplaincy is about. I will never forget what my battalion commander said when asking why I was so tired one day. Normally I was full of energy and enthusiasm for my work, but that day I seemed to be dragging. I said to him, "A young woman called last evening and said they were having serious family problems and needed to talk with me immediately. I tried to get them to come the next day, but it was very serious and extremely urgent, so I met them at 2 A.M. at the chapel." My CO quipped, "What could be *that* urgent?" I said, "They were struggling with a serious moral problem that was disintegrating their marriage. They were both ready for help then, and I was glad to be able to assist them—for their marriage was saved, and even more important, they both put Christ first in their own personal lives and in their marriage." Just sharing the story with him energized me and lifted my spirits the rest of the day. I thank God that in crisis counseling many are hungry to know God's Son as well as to resolve deep personal problems.

People who wear the uniform are looking for the same things we are looking for back home. The Christians are looking for fellowship, growth, and opportunities to serve right where they are. There is an enormous advantage a chaplain has over those in the civilian field of ministry. He lives and works alongside those who are not Christians. Some people come knocking on his door just wanting to relate to him as a person. Often the opportunities come without any effort on his part. On board ships and on the flight line, the chaplain can model the life of Christ to the men. Indeed, it is a ministry far removed from the religious symbolism of traditional churches. It is an immersion in a thoroughly secular and often cynical world. That is where Christian ministry needs to take place.

Eighty percent of the people in the armed forces are under 30 years of age. These are years when their value systems are being formed. Many of them come into the military disillusioned with society's institutions—especially the church. Like many people their own age, they complain about the church's irrelevance and hypocrisy while at the same time still having strong ties to it.

A chaplain's life sensitizes him to opportunities in everyday places. There is great value in his being visible on their turf, just as God in Christ was to us on our turf.

Stuart Barstad, former chief of chaplains of the United States Air Force, says, "Ministry is what matters. . . . Being present and available to minister to people in loss and pain, standing with them in the darkness and pointing toward the light—these are the things that count."

Neil Stevenson, former chief of chaplains of the navy, points out with these words another aspect of being a chaplain: "The joy of ministering to the young adults in the military is that we stay young with them. And the danger of it is that we may die trying to keep up with them."

When a person in the military runs into problems or has questions that are not related to military matters, the chaplain is the one to whom he is often referred. It seems that if it is a matter no one else can solve, then he should go talk to the chaplain about it. I did not take this opportunity lightly. The service person who can no longer hear his family or pastor praying for his safety from danger feels lost and powerless. To him the chaplain becomes the embodiment of all that is high and holy. Families can pray that their spouses and children are strong and growing in their faith, but the chaplain must create an environment in which this comes about.

So the term *chaplain* means many things. No matter how you look at it, we are missionaries, we are pastors, we are those who stand in a unique gap and plead for the souls of men and women as we touch the lives of military members at the point of crisis. This position offers opportunity for an innovative ministry and provides a chance to teach about the Savior to some who might not have listened when they were back home.

4

Forward into Battle

At Fort Campbell, Ky., the experience of being a hospital chaplain for the 71st Evacuation Hospital was waiting for me—who couldn't even stand the smell of hospitals! Just the thought of the trauma treatment center with its blood and surgery made me sick. But God was leading as He had in the past.

It wasn't long after associating with 101st Division's Chaplain Holland Hope that I spotted what I considered to be the ultimate ministry. I wanted to join the Screaming Eagles, the men of the 101st Airborne Division. The chance came, and I literally jumped at it.

At Airborne School, Ps. 104:3 took on new meaning. It talks about God walking on the wings of the wind and making the clouds His chariots. After three grueling weeks, I completed the final parachute jump to qualify. Then came the assignment to the "above the rest" battalion, the 327th Infantry. I had no idea what was in store by being committed to accompany this exciting outfit.

One short year after returning from Germany, our family moved again. This time it was so that we could be close to Doris's folks. Her parents were retired from the military and so knew the extreme pressure and loneliness experienced by military wives. The move there was made necessary because I was to deploy for a secret destination. I flew out of Nashville to San Francisco and boarded a ship. To my astonishment, it was the U.S. Navy ship *Eltinge*, the same one on which I had traveled to Germany 14 years earlier.

Life on board a crowded ship with men on their way to battle is both challenging and humbling. Talk about a place for ministry—it was alive and well on that ship. Even though the environment was not conducive to ministry, we were able to see much good come about in those crowded conditions. We had wall-to-wall captains, 12 officers stacked 3 high in our stateroom. All of us got along well together even among sister battalions, for we were all on a common mission. We knew we really needed each other and would rely on the man next to us for strength and security. The rapport built in tranquil and more nostalgic moments was useful to me to help minister to them when we together experienced the fear, hardship, frustration, and boredom of jungle combat.

God didn't wait for us to get out there in the jungle to do His work among the men. The winds of the Spirit were moving across the still waters of the South Pacific in a beautiful way. Numerous young men were making decisions to accept and serve Christ while they had time to reflect seriously on the unknown and the distinct possibility that they might never see their homeland again. Little did we realize that the 101st Airborne Division, one of the first to arrive in Vietnam and the last to leave, would sustain more casualties than the 101st did in all of World War II. There were four chaplains on board that ship, but only three returned. While living with the men under these difficult circumstances, my thoughts reflected on some of the history of the chaplaincy in the military.

The Army Chaplaincy traces its history to July 29, 1775, when the Continental Congress officially authorized the assignment of chaplains to military units. Gen. George Washington had 179 chaplains in his army, some for a few days, others for a full eight years. Three of them died in battle. Others were wounded, and some died of illnesses contracted in the field. Stories abound of the bravery and unselfish service of chaplains down through the years.

On the icy North Atlantic off Greenland during World War II, four American chaplains made a common sacrifice that moved the nation. Two Protestant, one Catholic, and one Jewish chaplain were on the *Dorchester,* a troopship that took a torpedo about four o'clock one morning. Terrified men groped out of the inky-black compartments. Many were without their

Chaplain Alexander conducting one of three
daily services on the way to Vietnam.

life jackets. The chaplains standing on the deck gave up their own life jackets to some of the men. They linked arms together and prayed the Lord's Prayer as the ship went down. Chaplain Clark Poling, one of the Protestant chaplains who went down on the *Dorchester,* had written to his father, "I know I shall have your prayers, but please don't pray that God will keep me safe. War is dangerous business. Pray that God will make me adequate."

Chaplain Kapaun was captured in Korea. He was an inspiration to the troops who refused to be brainwashed. He died after six months in captivity. He was a symbol of something Chinese Communists could not kill. Even though his body was dumped in a mass grave, they were still afraid of him. For a full year the prisoners wanted to have a memorial service, but the Communists refused to let them do it.

On board this ship we conducted morning devotions, noon prayer meetings, and evening vesper services. We also led many Bible studies in those 21 days it took us to get to Vietnam.

The question that was most often asked on that journey toward a battlefield was "Can I be a Christian and still kill?" The men asking were sincere soldiers who were being thrust into a real combat zone. Most of them had never known the reality of war except for what they had seen in films and on television. We were essentially men of peace, but now we were preparing to lean our faces into the winds of war.

The questions those men asked on that crowded ship are questions often debated in hallowed halls of sacred learning. But it was not ours to have the luxury of such a setting. We were wrestling to find the real flesh-and-blood answers. They were not philosophical for us.

Matt. 5:44 commands us, "Love your enemies." We can love our enemies, but if our enemies are criminals and about to assault our spouse, our children, or our parents, will we allow the criminals to commit such a vicious crime?

A search of the Bible reveals many references that have to do with peace and war, loving and killing. It seemed that the more we looked at the Scripture, the less simple the answers became with regard to the place of the soldier in the Christian community. As I traveled with these men across the blue Pacific, we struggled with some of these life-and-death issues both from the point of Scripture and from our real-life, everyday experience. We may not have arrived at any great or grand conclusions, but we did come face-to-face with some realities that life had never asked us to consider before this time. If there are good things that come out of wars and battlefields, one of them surely must be helping the people who are in them realize that life's issues are at one and the same time complicated and simple.

In today's world, where religious freedom would be the first liberty to vanish if we backed out on our responsibility to defend it, the Christian, whether military or civilian, must ask these serious questions as well. Certainly those who have relatives in the military or are there themselves have to deal with them.

In the Vietnam era, the separation that existed between the military and civilian communities had some ill effects. Because of this separation, some service men and women lost their motivation to make personal sacrifices. On the other hand, the civilian populace tended to look upon the soldier as less than a citizen.

Thankfully, this is changing since the Persian

Gulf War of 1991. Desert Storm, with its potential for heavy casualties, brought America to her knees in prayer. Our communities and churches kept in touch with servicemembers and gave them a heroes' welcome back home. May we never forget those who continue to sacrifice for their country.

The Vietnam conflict, which we were just entering as we made our journey across the Pacific, had the added dimension of a divided nation. It was no longer a simple division between the pacifists and those who believed war could be justified. It was between those who felt *this* war was immoral and those who defended freedom just as they had during wars earlier in our history.

So as our ship cut its way through the ocean waves, we waded through the pages of the Old and New Testaments, looking at the Scriptures to find some answers for the situation we were certain would face us when we reached those distant shores.

What exactly does the sixth commandment mean when God declares, "Thou shalt not kill"? Is there a difference between murder and killing? Certainly the men who were going into battle would have little choice between killing and being killed. How about King David, who was forbidden to build the Temple because he was a man of war? Were we as soldiers somehow of lesser value because we were going to defend our country?

The New Testament speaks on various occasions of centurions, officers commanding 100 Roman soldiers. Three of these are noted here. Our Lord said one of these had great faith, greater than He had found in Israel (Matt. 8:5-13; Luke 7:2-10). Another acknowledged at the foot of the Cross that Christ was the Son of God (Matt. 27:54; Mark 15:39; cf. Luke

23:47). The third was the first person to receive the baptism of the Holy Spirit as a Gentile (Acts 10). There is no indication that Jesus condemned them for their vocation any more than John the Baptist did in Luke 3:14, when he inferred theirs was a lawful profession.

These tough airborne soldiers asked probing questions about Matt. 5:39: "What about turning the other cheek, Chaplain?"

The only answer I could give them was that entering into combat is a kind of turning the other cheek. You're letting the enemy smite your cheek rather than those you love.

Rom. 12:18 is valid: "If possible, so far as it depends on you, be at peace with all men" (NASB). Many soldiers knew and asked about this scripture. However, the aggressor himself removes the probability of peace unless we surrender. This was the dilemma of the men who found themselves up against the enemy in Vietnam. History shows that if we appease an aggressor, or the bully on the block, or a Hitler, we only encourage more aggression.

What about "no sword"? Even Jesus at one time reminded His followers to buy a sword (Luke 22:36). Just because Peter misused the sword doesn't invalidate this teaching (John 18:10-11). Those who rely solely on the sword instead of God's teaching will certainly perish (Matt. 26:52).

As we look back at the history of our nation, it is clear that our religious and political liberties are enjoyed because our forefathers struggled and fought for them. The Liberty Bell proclaimed our independence, but Valley Forge and Yorktown won it for us.

Some would say that war blights the character of men morally and spiritually. That is only half true. It is true that war may mean destruction, debt, and carnage, but the virtues of patriotism, duty to others, selfless courage, and self-sacrifice come to the forefront as people are thrust together to preserve precious freedoms. Under combat stress, we tend to look to the real values in life—the spiritual and moral values. Life is stripped down to its bare essentials.

In looking at these men on that ship, I was proud to be identified with this group, who believed enough in the freedoms they enjoyed to offer to lay down their lives for the preservation of those freedoms. It is well for our nation to feel that same emotion of gratitude and pride in them. As I joined the other chaplains in holding daily worship services and teaching Bible studies, my heart became heavy for each of the men on board. I would be standing between them and the Cross, between life and death itself. Some of the last words they would hear would be mine. It was a scary responsibility, and yet it was an honor to stand with them.

On board the *Eltinge* life was not exactly paradise. To make matters worse, we were not even privileged to stop off a few days in Hawaii. There was fresh water to drink, but not enough for bathing. We washed our clothes by throwing them over the side of the ship, letting them bounce in the wake, and hauling them back up. Needless to say, it didn't help the appearance of the fragile jungle fatigues.

Finally the long journey was over, and we arrived in Cam Ranh Bay, Vietnam. The tropical heat was stifling and overwhelming. We stayed on board ship the first night. Periodically the guards would throw percussion grenades down over the side in case a Vietcong frogman should come and attach an explosive charge to try to blow up the ship in the harbor. The next day we took our jeeps and equipment off the huge transport ship and started our trek inward. An early patrol set out on foot with a German police dog along. They had gone only a few miles when the dog died from the heat.

5

Ministry Under Fire

The reality of war descended on us quickly. One night some snipers got into our midst and shot two of our men. They were sent to the hospital in Nha Trang. I soon learned that hospital visits were going to be a major part of my mission. I went to see not only them but others by the score later on when we engaged the Vietcong more frequently.

Cam Ranh Bay was a beautiful place. Such contrast could easily be seen—striking beauty and abject poverty. The mountains across the bay rise in majestic beauty, and yet the poverty of the people was overwhelming to us. What a shame, I thought, that those beautiful mountains are so infested with men at war. I felt grateful to be part of a nation that was so affluent and where children could receive so many extras in life. I felt sorrow for those people who seemed to lack even the necessities of life. There appeared to be a hollowness and a distrust in their eyes. Of course, if armies had rampaged across America as they had Vietnam, perhaps we, too, would look and feel the same. I wanted to share our affluence and the good news of Jesus Christ and how He could make a difference in their lives and in their country. However, many of them had peace and were content with few material things. I would soon be impressed with the dynamic faith and courage of many Vietnamese Christians and American missionaries who stayed with them in the midst of grave danger and hardship.

Our mission here was to set up a base camp providing security for the port complex. Sooner or later I felt I would have to accompany the men on offensive operations. But right now I was preoccupied with more mundane things. What one wouldn't have given for some ice cream and cold milk! We became used to good chow on board ship, but that was nowhere to be found on shore. As the reality of being in a combat zone settled down upon me, I began to feel sorry for myself.

Having never served in combat before, I began to think and pray about my style of ministry in this unique situation. On one of our first operations in Vietnam, I settled on the kind of ministry I felt would help me identify closely with the troops. Rather than staying in a base camp and waiting for them to come back from their operations, I decided to go out with them on as many operations as was physically and emotionally possible. Of course, I was not required to do this by any military orders. One of the sergeants pointed this out one day after we had had an especially difficult hot climb up a hill on a reconnaissance patrol. "Chaplain, you don't have to be here like we do, but we really appreciate your coming along with us." I prayed that the Lord would open the door to minister to the combat troops as I walked with them on their turf. It gave me a good understanding of what they were experiencing. God answered prayer.

The idea of walking with others on their own turf really started with the illness of our son Bill in Germany. One morning about 5 A.M. Doris went in to check on his breathing, which was labored due to bronchitis and asthma. Suddenly she called, "Curt, something is wrong with Bill!"

I ran into the room and saw that he had stopped breathing. His face was already starting to turn blue. I gathered him quickly in my arms, bounced down four flights of stairs, ran across the street in my bare feet in the dead of winter to the dispensary, kicked open the door, and screamed at the top of my lungs, "Medic!" The doctor came out and with calm assurance and presence of mind reached into his throat and pulled out the mucus and phlegm that had caused him to stop breathing.

We were concerned for quite some time about losing our son. We guarded him and helped him as much as we could, but the fevers and illness still came. We even thought of asking about a transfer to get out of Germany to a drier climate, but we felt this was where God wanted us. Our ministry was going well, and we trusted the Lord and brought Bill to Him in prayer.

One of the treatments the doctor prescribed was that whenever our child's fever would get above 103 degrees, we were to put him in a bathtub with cold water. So we would fill it with ice water and put the little lad in there to bring his fever down. As we did this, of course, Bill would kick and cry and resist. But if we hadn't bathed him in it, there would have been no way to reduce his fever and save his life. On one occasion I was sharing this story with one of our lieutenants. He said, "Our son is having trouble with high fevers too. I felt the same way you do about the process of bringing his fever down. Finally I decided to walk into the shower with him and turn the cold shower on both of us."

That was convicting, for here was the secret of identification, of walking together in love. It was an illustration of what Jesus did for us when He left heaven to become a part of us in order to understand our temptations and trials, our hurts and weaknesses. So I decided to do that with Bill. The next time we filled the bathtub and put the ice cubes in, I sat in it and shivered along with him. It wasn't pleasant. I suffered too, but I could identify with him, and he seemed to understand that his father was willing to go through the same thing he had to endure.

I wanted to do the same in Vietnam, to identify with the troops and understand them. I wanted to know where they were coming from—to endure their hardships, to experience their dangers, to walk with them as much as possible. It was important to be a chaplain to all the personnel, in the support groups as well as to those going forward into the battle area. So I would stay out with the troops for weeks at a time, joining them as they slept on the ground with no tents over their heads. That ministry produced tremendous dividends in getting to know the men by name and becoming a shepherd who knew his sheep. This kind of life took its toll, but it produced closeness with the men and love for them and giving the best possible ministry to them. After a while, they began to expect me to walk with them.

This ministry of presence paid off as the opportunities came to share Christ with both the officers and enlisted men. One officer in particular comes to mind; his name was Bob. He had shared some of his feelings in the ship's cabin on the journey across the ocean. Because he was such a huge man, probably 6 feet 6 inches tall, he felt that the Vietcong could not help but zero in on him, and he might not come back. He was the father of six children. We had dinner together with his family just before we left Fort Campbell. As we talked on the ship, I tried to lead him to Christ but with no success. One hot afternoon, while we were traveling up the An Khe Pass, I went over to talk to Bob. He was busy planning an operation with the battalion commander, but he excused himself to share some great news.

"Chaplain, you don't have to worry about me anymore. I have found the Lord, and He's very real to me. Everything is OK. Your prayers are answered. I'm not fighting God anymore. I prayed for Him to take me back to Him. I've experienced His forgiveness. Thanks for your concern and prayer."

The next day my emotions were overwhelming as I looked down on his lifeless body, riddled with machine-gun bullets. How grateful I was that we could write his wife and assure her and their six children that Bob had told of his having received Jesus the day before he was killed. He was one of the diplomat warriors of the 101st and one of the first officers to fall in battle.

During that same major battle I conducted services for one of the companies that had been alerted to go in and help relieve Bob's battalion. I had a great liberty and sensed the power of the Holy Spirit as we shared briefly in worship. When we sang that great invitation hymn "Where He Leads Me I Will Follow," battle-hardened Platoon Sergeant Dixon stepped forward and knelt in the dust. Salty tears washed down, making rivulets through the accumulated dust on his cheeks. Were there others who would follow him? The men were challenged not to come unless they really meant business, but it was like trying to hold back the wind with one hand. The wind of God's

Spirit was moving with refreshing conviction. They knelt in a semicircle five and six deep in front of the jeep. What a sight! One could almost hear the angels harmonizing in praise.

Soon after this, a platoon from a cavalry unit that had been on an extended screening mission in that same operation called on the radio, reporting they had not had an opportunity for worship in weeks. They wondered if I could come out and conduct a worship service. It was a vital opportunity to go and preach to these men hungry for the gospel. However, when we flew over the small hill where they were dug in for the night, the pilot said, "Chaplain, it's getting dark and I can't land; the hill is too steep. You will have to jump off the helicopter and stay there."

He hovered over that small hilltop with one strut about 5 feet off the ground and the other about 20 feet off the ground. I jumped out with the ammunition box that held my Bible and songbooks. Except for the men guarding the perimeter, the entire platoon assembled for worship. I suggested they sing loudly enough for the Vietcong to hear us, knowing they were all around us in the jungle. They sang with great gusto and enthusiasm. No doubt the Vietcong heard something so unknown to their concept of battle that they could not comprehend it. Perhaps that is why we walked off the hill the next day without a fight. They may have sensed that any American unit that sings before combat would be a formidable foe. I thought of the Old Testament story about the Levite choir singing before the soldiers and God taking care of the enemy (2 Chron. 20:1-30).

It was a miserable night, but I will never forget the kindness of one of the second lieutenants and a sergeant. They said, "It's raining and you don't even have a poncho. Why don't you join us? We have two ponchos held up about two feet by branches on the side of the hill."

We slept on what little bit of grass we could find. The poncho kept at least part of the rain off our faces and bodies that night. The men seemed deeply grateful that a chaplain was willing to go to them, bring them a worship service, and stay all night with them while knowing full well the possibility of being overrun by the enemy. Twenty years later that platoon leader, now an LTC and an instructor at the armor school at Fort Knox, confronted me. He said, "Curt, I've never forgotten that experience." It was another way for a minister in uniform to identify with his congregation in a unique way, bonding himself to his people.

Another good thing that came out of the battlefield experience was the rising to the surface of a spir-

A refugee youngster being
carried by his mother
from the battle scene.

Our battalion surgeon and a medical aid
team treating Vietnamese in the village.
I accompanied them and held up a baby
on the right. These posters were displayed in many cities,
showing the 101st as not only warriors
but also men of compassion.

it of genuine compassion and mercy. This was true,
not only when their buddies were wounded or needed help, but also as the men looked about them to the
people who were native to this land. Even in the field
services men would come up afterward and hand
over some money, saying, "Chaplain, make sure this
helps the people of Vietnam. Help the orphans, those
whose churches have been devastated, and the mountain people who are so poor and have so little."

Men of compassion do not lose their sense of caring for one another even in battle. In fact, it may
heighten the sense of values that says the best thing to

51

do with one's life is to give it away. They saw the needs firsthand.

This characteristic of American soldiers has strengthened our nation and churches tremendously through the years. You can see it firsthand on many world mission fields. Our servicemembers have helped build churches around the world. Now a quarter of a century later, we are reaping the positive benefits of Christian men being in Vietnam during that terrible war. Churches all across the country are opening their arms of compassion to a people they never would have heard about had it not been for courageous men going to serve in an unpopular war.

In Vietnam they saw the work of missionaries firsthand. Many of the missionaries were killed, and some were captured. Just as in all the terrible events in the history of the world, God is at work turning them around to bring glory to His name in spite of man's inhumanity to man. His love really does win out after all.

There was another thing that could be observed about troops in the heat of the battle: It sorted out those who had faith from those who did not. In battle, strength of will is needed to withstand the ordeal. A vital faith in God gives confidence that the goal can be obtained. In combat, stress eats away and breaks down the will. Faith strengthens the will. It gives the soldier an additional reason for not failing. When such reasons as family ties, personal pride, and pride in the particular unit are not enough, faith in God sustains.

During the early years of the war in Vietnam, we had very little problem with drugs but did have some with alcohol. Drugs did become a serious problem, however, as the war dragged on. The problem arose

A proud mother showing off her newborn baby to me.

partly because of the lack of will of our nation to support the war effort. This had the causative effect of deteriorating the will of the fighting troops in Vietnam and led to greater drug and alcohol abuse.

The positive impact of a man's faith was evident as wounded men were brought into the hospital. The men with strong faith in God seemed to be able to take the pain and suffering more easily. They really were something special. Something extra seemed to be a part of their lives. They were truly "a cut above the rest."

Don't misunderstand. The pain and suffering of battle wounds is terrible. Coming back from the combat zone and visiting the men in the hospital made it more difficult to go out again, especially as one sees with his eyes and experiences with his soul the pain

Time out for some green tea with a
friendly family on an operation.

and agony these men were going through. Some
would be maimed for life through what a land mine
or a bamboo spike (pungi stake) could do. The results
of a machine-gun or AK-47 bullet that has ripped
through the flesh and broken the bones of a soldier is
horrible to see.

But the call to the battlefield still rang in my heart
as I watched the men go. So, many times I would answer the call for a service somewhere in the combat
zone. With the scenes from the hospital fresh in mind,
it was not difficult to become very intense while
speaking to the men who stood on the forward edge
of the battle area. It was imperative to lift up Jesus, to
speak the words that would make a difference in their
lives and in where they would spend eternity.

In the dense jungle we really got down to the ba-
sics of the ministry. Worship and fellowship happen

as real and meaningfully under an open sky with green jungle around as in a beautiful stained-glass chapel. More often than not, the chapel consisted of a field altar placed on the front end of a jeep and men just sitting around in relaxed positions. It might be the deck of a ship, an open field, a steamy tarmac on an airfield, or somewhere else. The setting varies, but the ministry does not. We were there to care for our men. Men of many denominations were ours to minister to on the forward edge of the battle area. They included Protestants, Catholics, Jews, atheists, agnostics, and those who could not care less about Christ or religion of any kind.

You have heard the old cliché "You can lead a horse to water, but you can't make him drink." Not true! If you feed him salt, he'll drink. Jesus talked in Matt. 5:13 about Christians being the salt of the earth. Where can one find a better place to be the salt of the earth than in the combat zone with people who face great crisis and challenge? We tried to be the salt to make men thirsty for the water of life.

Much of the time as chaplains we served individually. Giving out continually, we felt the need for support from other chaplains. We felt like very small grains of salt. Though it was extremely difficult to get together, I nevertheless made occasional opportunities for fellowship with the other brigade chaplains, Bob Harlee, George Alexander, and Bill Barragy, for my own spiritual well-being.

Of course not every day was spent in some kind of battle experience. There were many days and sometimes weeks on end when life was pretty routine. One of the great difficulties in Vietnam was that the battle area was difficult to define and often more difficult to find. So we learned to live through the routine everydayness of war. It was Fleet Admiral Nimitz who in 1946 said his esteem for the chaplain was not so much placed upon deeds of valor as it was upon appreciation for their routine accomplishments.

One day when things were especially slow, my chaplain's assistant and I heard a firefight break out on one of our platoon's search-and-destroy missions not far from where we were bivouacked. I suggested, "Let's go out and find out what's going on. Maybe they need us out there."

Little did we realize what was about to happen. My assistant covered me with his M-16 rifle as we walked out through one little village and into the rice paddies. Following the bursts of small-arms fire, we approached the location. After we crossed a river, I knew we were not on the safest ground, but I figured our men were only a short distance away. I thought we could find them, but the farther we went, the farther away the battle sounded. Before we knew it, we were lost in hostile territory and came into a small village. As we came around one hut, three men dressed in black pajamas with weapons confronted us. We had a kind of standoff. My chaplain's assistant was ready to defend with his M-16, but there were three of them. We looked at each other, not knowing if they were friend or foe. We tried to communicate in Vietnamese, of which I knew very little. I gave them a greeting and then thought to ask if they were Catholic or Protestant (at least knowing those words). They said they were Catholics and showed their crucifixes. I thought, They are probably friendly and not Vietcong. Later I remembered there were Catholics and Protestants among the Vietcong. We backed out of the village and turned the other way. Providentially, nothing happened. That episode was enough for my assistant and me to hightail it back to the safety of our own perimeter. We quickly crossed back over the river and saw the battalion commander standing there. "Where have you been?" he asked in colorful language.

We told him we were out trying to find a platoon in a firefight. He said they had just returned a few minutes ago, and they were about ready to send out a search party for us. The commander was angry. "Don't ever do that again!" he warned. He didn't have to tell us a second time. From then on we stayed as close to our troops as possible, never venturing out alone.

God took us through some dangerous spots in those months with the troops in Vietnam. On one occasion we were walking as a unit through the jungle. The man in front of me yelled in pain, as he had walked into a pungi stake in the high grass. A pungi stake is a piece of bamboo sharpened and dipped in animal or human feces to cause infection, which could result in amputation or death. The VC hid these devious devices in the tall grass or among jungle trails. Some of our men were killed by land mines hidden in the same manner.

On another occasion we conducted a platoon memorial service for men who had been killed a few days earlier in a firefight with the Vietcong. When we had finished, I walked out the front door of the building. Some of the men went out the back door. As they did, there was a deafening explosion. Another man had stepped on a land mine, and we called in a helicopter to take him to a hospital.

Once I went out to visit one of our companies and was running to get into a sampan, a little Vietnamese boat with room enough for only two people.

The idea was to get across the flooded rice paddy before it got too dark and get back to the jeep and the comparative safety of our command post. As I ran along the village path, one of the fellows spoke out in a commanding voice, "Hold it, Chaplain!"

There's room for only one American
in a two-man Vietnamese sampan,
as I discovered by crowding into this one.

I stopped suddenly, and he said, "I was just kidding you, but I wanted to slow you down because there are still land mines around here."

The next day they found a land mine a few feet from where he had told me to stop. Many other times God kept me safe. Once I almost got on a helicopter that crashed just over the hill. Another time I was in a rice paddy, and we took sniper fire. I followed close behind the platoon sergeant in that operation.

Just before Christmas in a major war zone area

near Saigon I was talking with a soldier when all of a sudden a shot rang out. A sniper had shot him in the head. We both fell to the ground, and as I looked over, I saw a bullet hole in his helmet. Yet he was smiling! I couldn't believe what I saw. The bullet had penetrated the outer steel shell of the helmet and ricocheted around the outside of the fiberglass lining. It gave him a ringing headache for three days, but he was a grateful man.

As we were lying there on the ground, I looked over and saw what looked like a round radio speaker, and I said to the sergeant, "What is that thing over there?"

He said, "You'd better stay down there, Chaplain, and call for someone to come over and check it out."

It turned out to be a Chinese Communist land mine that would have wiped out all of us at one time had the enemy been there to detonate the thing.

6

Beyond the Call of Duty

The combat experience I recall most vividly happened on my birthday. I was with a platoon of men called the Tiger Platoon, along with a task force from the battalion command post. Our mission was to relieve one of our sister companies pinned down by a North Vietnamese regiment.

We found them just after we crossed a bombed-out bridge where we saw dead water buffalo in what was once a beautiful stream. The smell of death was everywhere. As we joined the other company, small-arms fire was being exchanged, with fierce casualties on both sides. On the opposite edge of the battle area, Bravo Company was maneuvering into position. We were surrounded by clumps of bamboo and open fields. The area was best described as dried-up rice paddies. The enemy was dug in among the bamboo.

All of a sudden the commander of the Tiger Platoon, Lt. Jim Gardner, spoke into the radio: "Sir, we can't dislodge them. We are going to charge." The commander said, "Go!"

They got up from their positions, about 20 or 30 of them, and charged across 100 yards of open field—across that hard unplowed rice paddy. Under the withering fire of the enemy, men were rapidly falling to the ground. Some of them made the rice paddy embankment and were safe, at least for the time being.

As I looked out at those wounded men, I wondered how we were going to get them out of there. Some were already trying to crawl to safety, but others couldn't move at all. I said to the commander, "We need to get those guys out of the direct fire."

Since everybody else was busily engaged in fighting and there was only one medic available, the commander asked, "Do you want to try?" He offered me a rifle, but I declined. I could hear the crack of bullets overhead. I was so scared that my mouth was as dry as cotton, and I could hardly swallow.

As I crawled over the rough, plowed field that had not seen rain in many months, my jungle fatigues were torn to shreds. I didn't think I could make it at all, yet as I moved back and forth God helped me pull all 11 of those wounded men out of there. I left my web belt with two canteens attached, and when I got back from pulling the last wounded man out, I noticed that one of the wounded guys had drunk all my water. I kidded him for emptying the last drop of water from my canteens, but he surely needed the water more than I did. Later we were able to go back for the bodies of the 2 men who were killed.

One man was so far out in front of the others that we had difficulty reaching him. My efforts to get him out were unsuccessful. He was too badly wounded to be dragged out by one person. He was shot through the throat and in the chest. So I went back and asked for three volunteers. We tried to lift him up with a poncho under him, and in our haste to lift him I stood up, exposing my back to the North Vietnamese. But, miracle of miracles, instead of being shot, I got away without a scratch. We got him out OK.

It was here where Lieutenant Gardner was fighting. It was amazing to see him holding his helmet on top of his weapon over the rice paddy dike to draw enemy fire. He threw hand grenades when he thought he had located the source of fire. Lieutenant Gardner was killed later that day. Some of his men went out and found him and brought him back that night. I put a poncho over him and lay there on the ground under my poncho with mosquitoes buzzing around. The smell of death and blood was everywhere. He was only a couple of feet away. He had only one bullet in his heart and died with a smile on his face. Jim was later awarded the Medal of Honor posthumously for conspicuous gallantry in action. He led his platoon across the rice paddy and exposed himself to enemy fire, helping establish a beachhead there.

Now we had to figure out a way to get them evacuated from the battle area to the hospital before the enemy could overrun our position that night or before they died from lack of medical attention.

Lieutenant Den Foley took over the Tiger Force and continued to gallantly lead his troops. I've always had a special place in my heart for these men who sacrificed so much on the forward edge of the battle area. Unfortunately, they took heavy casualties in this action and others to follow.

It was at times like that under intense stress of the battle that one really gained an admiration for the chopper pilots. We prepared a landing zone for them to come in on and take out the wounded. As they zoomed in, they were being fired at with heavy-caliber machine guns. The green tracers were lighting up the sky over my head as I stood in the open field to guide them in. A young lieutenant, weary with the killing, shouted, "Get back here, Chaplain. There's been enough men killed!" Those pilots certainly risked their own lives as they became sitting ducks in the sky in order to come in for the rescue.

Thousands of miles away, at that precise time, a seminary professor's daughter, Marilyn Rose, felt an urgency to get up in the night and pray for me. She had been thinking about me and sensed I must be in extreme danger. Also that same night a neighbor of my wife felt the same compulsion and was awakened in the night, feeling I was in danger. God in His faithfulness was taking care of me.

The next morning we called in dive bombers to dislodge the enemy. We had already lost about 35 men killed in action and many more wounded. The planes came in parallel to us. That wasn't so bad, but then they came in at right angles, and one could see the bombs being released from their wings wavering right over our heads and striking about 150 meters from our position. The earth shook as we hunched down in our foxholes to avoid the shrapnel. Once again God spared our lives.

Later I walked through the carnage where our sister company had taken the brunt of the casualties. The results were very evident of their being caught in grazing fire from the enemy. Even when they lay down flat on the ground, they were caught in such low, devastating gunfire in that open, windswept rice paddy, it was almost impossible to escape alive. Many of them were killed with head wounds. One young man had grasped a tuft of grass and died an excruciating death. His face was contorted and twisted with pain. I wept freely while standing over him and praying for his spouse and the family he left behind. I still remember his face today.

Farther on, a North Vietnamese captain lay dead,

his comrades being unable to carry him off before they retreated. I picked up his hand grenade and his leather officer's belt and looked through his wallet. There was a picture of his family back in North Vietnam, where he would never return. I prayed for them too and realized no hate for this man, only hate for the war that had brought us here to Vietnam. Feelings of sadness and grief swept over me while thinking about all the letters that would have to be written to families of men killed in battle and the many memorial services that would mark the end of a life wasted in war.

We stayed there the next night and another day. I went out on a reconnaissance mission with what was left of the Tiger Platoon. After returning, I discovered that General William Westmoreland had visited the battle area. They said, "Hey, Chaplain, the big general was here, and you missed him."

But I was at the right place with our men in another operation. They needed someone to be with them to encourage and comfort them as they grieved for the friends they had lost in battle.

Shortly after that, two young soldiers who had been assigned to an outpost were killed. They had broken one of the basic rules of combat. They were smoking and making too much noise. The enemy slipped in and threw some hand grenades. I heard the horrible blast while trying to get some much-needed sleep. The battalion surgeon, the executive officer, and I ran out to them in the darkness and tried to pick them up. I couldn't get hold of one of them. We had to get out of there quickly, for the same people who threw that grenade were close by. Finally I grabbed him and was able to pull him back. Then it became evident that his arm had been blown off at the shoulder, which was why it was difficult to pick him up. My heart was broken to see the mutilation of another of our young men who had come over to maintain the freedom of South Vietnam.

Four months later, while preaching to a small group of men, I noticed that the sergeant major and the battalion commander were in attendance. They didn't often come, so I thought it a bit unusual but was grateful to see them. At the close of this preaching service the commander came up with the sergeant major and said that he had an award for me. The sergeant major called, "Attention to orders," and under the blazing sun I was awarded the Silver Star for gallantry in action. I felt deeply honored yet unworthy. Tears flowed down my cheeks.

After receiving the medal, I stuck it in a pocket. I was honored and humbled at the same time—honored to have been recognized as having done ministry above and beyond the call of duty, and humbled because so many went unrecognized. They would never even talk about it. It was part of being a soldier, serving their nation and assisting one another through uncommon dangers.

That was by far the worst action I had seen in Vietnam. The rest of my tour was scattered with smaller actions here and there.

One of the elements I appreciated about the military long before the physical fitness craze became vogue in our country was the element of being all you can be for yourself and your country. It has caused me to try to maintain a lifestyle of physical fitness that will help me be all I can be and should be for my Lord. Even when we went back to the base camp and relaxed, our leadership kept the focus on physical fitness. After tossing and turning part of the night because of the heat, I didn't really like to hear the rough voice of the sergeant major telling us to get up and get ready for PT. The run around the perimeter was just what we needed to maintain peak combat efficiency, but I would groan along with the rest of the troops when confronted with this every other morning in base camp. I, as a chaplain, needed this as well as the Airborne Infantry. I sometimes wondered about the saneness of doing this in a combat zone, but I'm grateful for the superb Airborne leadership in this area. I believe they performed with excellence mainly because they stayed in shape and had a special comradery and espirit among themselves. Not only would they fight for their country, but also they wouldn't let their buddies down. It was imperative that they did their best to stay alive themselves and help their friends get home as well.

Sometimes I would preach as many as four or five times a Sunday. Then I would also hold services five or six times a week by going around to different units, trying to cover those that were not assigned a chaplain. Holding so many field services took its toll. I recall setting up a worship service inside the company perimeter and going around to the foxholes, telling the men that a worship service was going to be held. The intense heat under the tropical sun was physically draining. There was no shade in that area. One service found the men sitting on the ground and the field altar set up on ammunition boxes. I always tried to carry song booklets along and do some singing, for I loved to sing, and so did the men. That particular service I began to feel a rapid loss of strength. In the middle of the message I told them, "I'm sorry; I can't go any further unless I sit down for a minute or so. If you want to, you can go back to your positions." I sat down weak and nauseated. I was probably dehydrated but wanted to finish the message if possible.

I will never forget Sgt. Don Emil, who went to his tent and brought back his helmet filled with water. He took a washcloth and bathed my forehead and gave me a drink from his canteen. A cup of cold water given in Jesus' name never ministered any better. I accepted his ministry with deep emotion. It seemed that God was trying to speak concerning the need to let others minister to me. The sergeant and I were close friends from there on out.

Sometime later Sergeant Emil lost his leg when he stepped on an enemy land mine. He was medically evacuated back to the States. I saw him again after being reassigned to Fort Campbell. There he was so excited about getting people into the chapel service that he would walk on his crutches and his new artificial leg up and down four flights of barracks steps to invite the soldiers to chapel service.

Adding to the problems of intense heat and dehydration was the fact that when we did return from an operation, sometimes the only cold drink offered in abundance was beer. I once came back from an operation so dehydrated that I had to be helped off the helicopter and could barely get back into the tent. I yearned for some cold water. The brigade commander had told us we were going to have soft drinks to go along with the beer that had recently arrived on a supply ship. We had been eating C rations for 45 days. As soon as we got off the helicopter that evening, my only thought was getting some ice and having a big soft drink. As promised, there was enough ice and mountains of beer. I looked for a soft drink, but they were all gone—not one lone soft drink left. My heart sank with the thought, What am I going to do now?

I looked at that beer. Some of the guys were looking at me and saw it was a test. Now what's this chaplain going to do? Will he drink beer with no soft drinks left? He really looks wasted. He needs liquid. They all knew the water out of the five-gallon cans tasted terrible. It had a horrible metal taste. I had made my stand in terms of alcohol, so I thought to myself, You haven't drunk up to this time, so don't start it now. I walked over and got a piece of ice and put it into my canteen cup and poured the foul-tasting water from one of the big water cans into my cup and drank.

This was repeated over and over. Always plenty of beer but very few soft drinks. Finally I complained to the commander. I was speaking not just for myself but also for the troops. Even though some of the men drank beer, they wanted soft drinks, too, so they wouldn't overindulge when they were very thirsty. I began to pray for a solution to the alcohol problem.

Occasionally we would receive boxes of cookies from folks back home. One lady included a letter in the box and asked, "Is there any need? Please let me know. I will work my hardest to assist."

So I wrote back and said, "Yes, there is one thing you can do. Is there any way in the world you can get us additional soft drinks? We would appreciate it." Upon receipt of my letter that lady went directly to the Coca-Cola people and told them about our dilemma. They took immediate action, and within a month we had all the soft drinks we needed!

7

Life and Death on the Battlefield

There was a great difference between the fighting troops and the support troops. The warriors lived in the field all the time. They slept in tents or under the stars with only ponchos to keep the rain off and sometimes nets to help keep the mosquitoes away. The support troops in Saigon and other places usually lived in more comfortable quarters. The barracks had fans, and some even had air conditioning. While many suffered, others lived comparatively well until the Tet offensive. Then Saigon and many other camps became just as dangerous as the field.

On December 25, 1965, I wrote to Paul Skiles in Kansas City, servicemember's director for my denomination, telling him about some of the battles.

> We were sent into the jungle to engage and destroy these two Vietcong regiments. For some reason they decided not to stand and fight. They never showed themselves except to harass us with sniper fire and the ever-present booby traps. But on a trip up to the Michelin rubber plantation at Ben Cat on the infamous Route 13, their mines demolished three of our vehicles. Besides the five men who were killed, there were many wounded—some lost legs, one lost both legs above his

knees. Experiencing the horrors and anxiety of this type of warfare really makes you think soberly.

Ambush site on Rte. 13 next to a rubber plantation where some of our men were killed by a land mine.

A week before Christmas, after coming back from the jungle, God worked a miracle in the lives of many of the men. Though this is a hardship tour, I have seen God work in marvelous ways. As one would expect in combat, men's hearts are turned to the eternal verities of life and death.

However, this tour has been the most satisfying I have ever experienced. So far God has allowed me to go out in every major operation with the troops. At times I am just as frightened as the men are. The adrenaline works overtime. I believe that because I have been able to identify myself with these men, my ministry has been more successful. When one endures the hardships and subjects himself to the same dangers, the men take note of this. Psalm 91 has been very precious to me, and I share it with others. I felt a real satisfaction in my ministry when 21 men came forward to meet the Master at the conclusion of this last Sunday in Advent. Even though men are more tender in times of great danger and fear, I believe many of these decisions will be lasting. My greatest concern is to lead them on to deeper spiritual life. The men need much more nurture and help than one chaplain can give under the conditions we are presently experiencing. We are on the move so much.

I received a letter from the wife of one of the fellows killed on Route 13. She had just delivered their first and only baby. There were just a few days' difference between these events. Four days after they had received the telegram from the government telling about his death, they received a letter from Benny, written the night before he was killed. She was so thankful to God for that much. She wrote, "Chaplain, I wanted to know if you knew Benny and ever talked to him either in a religious manner or just in everyday conversation." Benny had attended my field service just before he was killed.

I received another letter from the parents of a young corporal who was killed in a rice paddy by "friendly fire." He had been in our chapel service, and the next day his company came under enemy fire in the rice paddy. They called in artillery, but unfortunately some rounds fell short, and he was killed.

He was an adopted son. His father was vice president and director of broadcast standards for a major broadcasting company. His dad and mother had a terrible time coping with his death. The letter from his father questioned:

I do not know where or when or if this will reach you because it has been a long time since Christmas, and I have been carrying your letter around, hoping I would find the time and words to express the deep appreciation of my wife and me for your message. I appreciate the interest you gave. Such efforts take valuable time. But let me tell you that if you could know the help your words bring, you would feel that you are the most rewarded man alive.

Most of my life I have lived in a coldly competitive world. The one purpose I had was to be able to raise a son who would love God, whom I had never really known, to serve his country, and honor himself. I guess I have taught too well or loved too much because when the hope of the years in the future were dissolved so quickly, I gave up. I have learned that nothing is so intolerable as someone else's sorrows. But I put this on you because I want you to know that for whatever reason the spirit of your words lifted us up.

It was unfortunate that I could not minister more to this man who was so deeply hurt by losing his son. I remember the day when he was so proud to attend the graduation of Airborne School and stand by as the airborne wings were pinned on his son. I shared in the family pride and the excitement of a young man who had achieved a memorable goal in life. He served with one of the best units in the United States Army until that fateful day when one of our rounds fell short and so quickly snuffed out his life.

Tragedy upon tragedy, and yet that seemed to be the normal course of the day as day went into week and the Vietnam War continued to roll along.

I cut out of a newspaper a letter that was written to General Westmoreland. It was from a 17-year-old widow whose 19-year-old husband was killed in Vietnam. It reflects a courage in the finest tradition. She showed an unusually mature recognition of her husband's desire to defend his way of life and his posterity.

Dear General Westmoreland,

I received your letter today and was surprised but pleased to get it, and I felt that I should write and tell you this. Tom and I were married only 17 days when he was shipped overseas. He left there on December 28. We were married one month and 24 days when he died. I loved Tom and know he died for a purpose. He told me over and over again to try to understand why he had to go.

I learned that Tom could have been deferred because he was the only one left to carry on the Devlin name. Now there is no one when his father dies. He said that he did not want to be deferred. It was his job and he had to do it. I understood and I loved him.

Tom was a brave man. I am proud of him. He said that he would rather fight the Communists in Vietnam and die if he had to than to let them come over here. He said if we didn't stop them now, it wouldn't be long until we would be fighting them at home.

Tom was only 19, I'm 17. We were young to get married, but it was what we wanted, and my parents agreed. We both knew that he might never come back alive, but we had such faith and hope that he would. I know that God had a reason for taking Tom, and I must accept this.

Since Tom's death, the people in our community have realized that the war isn't so far away anymore. Tommy was the first boy in Hopkins County to be killed in this war. I feel the same way Tom and all the guys over there feel toward the draft card burners and protesters. Tom and hundreds of guys like him are fighting and dying every day for them, for all of us here in America so that we can live in a free world. Why can't these people realize this?

I know that my husband didn't die in vain. He died for what he believed in, and I am proud that he stood firm on this. He was proud to be a paratrooper and to be able to do something for his country. Maybe that is the reason I loved him so much. He was a paratrooper all the way. I hope you don't mind my writing you this letter, but it was just something I felt I had to do and wanted to do.

May God watch over and protect you and all the men fighting there for America. I pray for all of you. Prayers can't help Tommy anymore. He is at peace now, and he is with God. But maybe they will help somebody.

After we had been there many months, some of the men came to me and said, "Chaplain, we've accepted Christ as Savior and Lord, and we would like to be baptized."

I found a stream—a rather fast-moving stream. I became somewhat concerned as I thought about what would happen if I lost anybody. There was an old mess sergeant, a great big hefty fellow, who wanted to be baptized. Instead of getting drunk and going into town and tearing up the bars and visiting the places of prostitution, he had become a Christian. He was a giant of a man—and couldn't swim.

I warned him before I dunked him under that the bottom was slippery and the water downstream was over our heads. I stationed men on the bridge and along the bank so that they could save him if I lost my grasp on him. We told him to grab the pilings of the bridge if he slipped and to hold on for dear life until we could get him out. By the grace of God, however, we got him baptized and out of the water without incident.

I hated to think that heaven's gatekeeper might have had to announce, "Sergeant Anderson up from

Vietnam." Then the other angels would ask if he was another casualty from Vietnam, that tragic war, and he would reply, "No, I drowned while being baptized by Chaplain Bowers."

Among the other people baptized was one each of Turkish, Greek, and German descent. It was a time of great rejoicing and blessing as we who were brothers in warfare became brothers in Christ.

The mess sergeant, third from right,
is a part of this baptismal group.
German, Greek, and Turkish backgrounds
are represented in these American fighting men.

Communion was a very worshipful, meaningful time to all of us. I remember dirty, grubby, battle-scarred hands reaching up toward heaven as I would gently place a wafer in each one. The men would take it with tears in their eyes, thanking God for keeping them safe thus far. We often sang with gusto:

Amazing grace! how sweet the sound
That saved a wretch like me!

75

Thro' many dangers, toils, and snares
I have already come.
'Tis grace hath brought me safe thus far,
And grace will lead me home.

—JOHN NEWTON

Some of them did go home—to their eternal home. Communion took on special significance for the combat soldier and for this chaplain who celebrated it often with heaviness in his own heart, yet with gratitude to Jesus, who drew near to us on the battlefield.

I respected more and more every day the fighting ability of the infantrymen, especially the airborne troops. On one operation I felt the grizzly hand of death upon hearing an explosion and running over to see three of our men lying there dead. Others were torn up badly. Twelve of them lay there severely wounded. One of these young men died in my arms. He was a Catholic fellow.

Some Catholic buddies came to me and said, "Father [knowing that I wasn't a priest], please give him last rites." Of course, I said a prayer over him and commended him into the hands of God, hoping that all was well with him before he went on to eternity. No matter what we could do, we couldn't do anything to save his life. He couldn't talk to me. All I could do was talk to him and tell him about the love of Jesus and hope he heard these last words.

One of the young men lying there, badly wounded, had accepted Christ not long before in one of the worship services. I had given him the book *Peace with God,* by Billy Graham. He wanted to be baptized.

He said, "Take this book, Chaplain." As he handed it to me, I noticed that it was full of shrapnel and had blood all over it. It had been read and reread until it was dog-eared. I had the privilege of baptizing him at the hospital.

We went out many times without even being fired upon. But on one occasion I was with a platoon sergeant going through a rice paddy. They were on a sweeping operation when shots cracked over our head. We all hit the mushy ground at the same time. The platoon sergeant started to fire and maneuver his platoon toward the snipers. I stuck close behind this seasoned veteran, who had fought in the Korean War and knew exactly what he was doing.

As we were running across the area, the men were firing and maneuvering, as well as trying to avoid the pungi stakes. Sergeant Oliver yelled at me, "Chaplain, when you jump across the stream, be careful. I just missed some pungi sticks there!"

When we got to the village, the snipers melted back among the villagers, and we couldn't tell the enemy from our friends. They hid their weapons and appeared to be nothing more than rice farmers. Sweaty, hot, discouraged, we cut that day's operation short and went back to base camp.

Although not liking to go out much at night, on one occasion I felt I should go along with one of the line companies. We left in the middle of the night. When they came by to wake me up, I was sleeping soundly. I didn't really want to get up and go. I was as afraid and tired as they were. Moving out quietly and carefully, we started out in single file across the fields and into the jungle. We weren't long in the jungle until the man in front of me turned around and said, "Chaplain, we've lost the column of men in front of us. We're lost."

I responded, "Don't worry. There's a radio man

back of us. We'll go back and get him to check on the front of the column." We found they had taken a right turn at one of the small ravines in the deep jungle.

While leading them into the ravine, I kicked up some fox fire (decayed vegetation that is luminescent and glows in the dark). I instructed the men, "Each of you take a piece and put it under your helmet band so that you can see the person in front of you. The Vietcong won't be able to see us from any distance, but we can avoid getting lost again." We looked like dancing ghosts bouncing through that dense, deep jungle in the middle of the night, but at least we were able to follow one another. Finally we ended up with the main column. None of us wanted to be lost out there. I had a fear of being captured in Vietnam when being out with the men. None of the chaplains captured in the Korean War came back alive. It was a great relief to rejoin the main group.

As we moved along through the jungle, shafts of light began to filter through the trees. As we came near our objective, the Vietcong camp was spotted by our reconnaissance patrol. Everybody got nervous and quiet, and about that time the man right in front of me screamed out in pain as he walked into a pungi stake. He lay there on the ground with blood coming from the calf of his leg. We called in a helicopter to medivac him out.

Farther up the trail we ran into another trap. Fortunately, we saw it before it got any of us. It was a long bamboo spear with a trip wire. Had we triggered it, one or two soldiers along the path would have been impaled. After that, we hacked our way through the jungle and stayed off the main trails.

When we arrived at the camp, all we found were smoking fires. The Vietcong had heard us coming and left as quickly as they could, leaving everything behind but their weapons. It started raining as we trudged ahead to find a landing zone where we could call in the choppers to get us back to our base camp. It poured, making us wet and cold. But within a few hours the sun came out and warmed us as we walked through the fields and the jungles. Somehow we lost our bearing, and the entire company was lost. We took turns chopping our way through the jungle with the machetes. Finally, at three o'clock the next morning, we were so exhausted we could go no farther. We set up a perimeter guard and lay down on the damp jungle floor for a few hours of sleep.

At dawn we struck off again and finally made radio contact with our battalion. They guided us into a helicopter landing zone, where they picked us up and took us back to the base camp. There I prepared my message to preach, again in the comparative safety of our support base.

There was no way that one could permanently stay out on combat operations without breaking down with battle fatigue. I thank the Lord for the base camp, where we could go back and rest and relax awhile.

In spite of what is indicated by Hollywood films, a human being cannot take constant contact with the enemy. The adrenaline cannot flow continually without irreparable damage to the emotional and physical life of soldiers. The combat troops endured in the jungle much longer than I, but anxiety and weariness had begun to take its toll on me as well. According to Chuck Dean in his book *Nam Vet*, more of our armed forces personnel who served in the Vietnam conflict have committed suicide since the end of the war than those who were actually killed there.

Our B-52s were called in to bomb a North Vietnamese position in the jungle west of Tuy Hoa. We were asked to assess the damage and see if they had hit the target. I went up to the mountains along with a company of men. The streams were so swift that we had to form a daisy chain (link arm in arm) in order to cross the mountain stream without being swept away. The Vietcong were everywhere, so we couldn't take time to bathe. We were so filthy we could not stand the smell of ourselves and wanted desperately to just linger and enjoy the scenery, the beautiful waterfalls, and the sparkling clear water.

That night we lay down in the jungle. The next morning when waking, I looked down and saw blood oozing from the top of one of my jungle boots. I took the boot off, and there was a big leech that had fastened itself to the calf of my leg. It was already bloated from sucking so much blood. We always had to look over each other after we had walked through the rice paddies because the leeches had to be removed. I didn't realize until then that they were everywhere.

The company remained in the area, and the commander sent a small patrol to assess the damage the American bombers had inflicted on the enemy in the jungle. I decided to go out with them. I felt scared through the entire episode and thought I really should not have been there with that small squad of only eight men. We found nothing but gaping holes where the bombs had dug out craters.

On our way back, we came upon an abandoned Vietcong camp. Their fires were still burning. They left in a hurry because they were not prepared to fight, nor did they have time to set up an ambush. I could picture the horror they must have felt when I saw a foxhole that had been extended deeper with bare hands the night those B-52 bombs landed on the hill on the other side.

We stayed on the forward edge of the battle area for almost a year. Later in the war, the staff chaplain in Saigon decided there was too much stress on a chaplain who was assigned to a combat unit for a full 12-month tour. He began to rotate chaplains from combat units to support units every six months. However, I had the chance to go to a support unit that was permanently located by Cam Ranh Bay on the South China Sea before that decision was made.

8

An Ever-present Presence

The mountains rose in majestic splendor as I stood on the sandy shores looking across Cam Ranh Bay. The temptation to accept the possibility of staying here instead of returning with our combat unit to battle was strong. Here I could have a tent only 100 yards from the South China Sea, right on the beach. Scuba diving in the coolness of the sea in the comparative safety of the port where supplies were being unloaded was a real luxury. There were plenty of men here who needed a ministry. At this point in the war a huge airstrip was being built for F-4 Phantom Jet fighters. But the call to stay with the men whom I had learned to respect and love as we walked together through the jungle, across the rice paddies, and into the forward edge of the battle area was more urgent than the temptation to take it easy for a while. I wanted to be with them as a constant reminder that the Lord Jesus loved them.

So it was back to the lifestyle of living in the jungle and having to put up with the inconveniences that were built into following the nomadic 101st Airborne. We went to a location near the Cambodian border, and had no place to set up, except in the dirt where a new airstrip was being dug out of the terrain. It was during the monsoon season. My personal quarters consisted of a cot with a poncho stretched over the foxhole. I shared this with my chaplain's assistant. We dug a hole big enough for two cots. This was our home for two weeks. When the rain came, water would drip into the foxhole, leaving about three to four inches of mud on the bottom. Then we would have to wait for the sun to dry it out.

My sleeping quarters on an exercise
near the Cambodian border.

Living in these physical conditions was hard on morale. The troops would come back muddy from an operation, only to sleep in a muddy place. It was wade in the mud, sleep in the mud, live in the mud, and eat food out of a steel mess kit with rain dripping from our helmets into the food.

While we were living under these conditions, a new general came in to take command. He was a good commander and anxious to get on with winning the war. It fell my duty to talk with him about the troops. It was necessary to tell him, "Sir, the morale is a lot lower than you realize. These men are tired and stressed. They have been in the jungle for nine months and have had little rest." That was not exactly what he wanted to hear, but I had to be honest with him and with the men I represented.

It was during this time that our brigade chaplain, a fine Catholic priest named Bill Barragy, was killed in a helicopter crash. He was flying in a Chinook chopper with about 25 other men. They were up close to the Cambodian border. At first we thought the crash was caused by ground fire, but it wasn't. It was a malfunction in the helicopter. The rotor blade bearing froze, causing the helicopter to rotate around the blades as it came crashing down to a fiery end. Upon hearing about it, I climbed in the command helicopter along with the battalion commander and flew over the crash site. There was a striking contrast between the dark green jungle and the white-hot fire from the burning magnesium.

A platoon of men cut their way through the jungle to see if there were any survivors. There were none. Twenty-five men along with Chaplain Barragy died. He was the first chaplain to be killed in Vietnam. Many others were to follow him. Needless to say, we missed this man very much in our brigade. Until a replacement came, the rest of us ministered to the Catholic men in his unit as best we could.

Some of the officers were not sympathetic to a

chaplain and his ministry. However, most of them were grateful for our presence. One ex-marine officer had a reputation for being a brave and daring leader and for taking excellent care of his men. Harry would not attend any of the services but faithfully put the word out when worship services were conducted for his troops. However, many times he would be found standing within earshot while his men were worshiping.

On one occasion he was standing a little closer than usual. I asked him, "Harry, what's going on? I thought you said you didn't want to go to my field services because you are not in sympathy with what I am preaching—the love of Christ and love of your neighbor."

"Naw, Chaplain, I don't want my men to get too loving. They have to be fighters, and I don't want them to get too much of this Christianity stuff."

I asked, "How come you have better attendance than any other platoon?"

He smiled to himself and responded, "I guess a little bit won't hurt them. I hear what you are saying from a distance, Chaplain. I just don't want the guys to think I'm getting soft."

Some months later I saw his body along with many others in a makeshift morgue. I wept because he was a man I loved and respected very much. I trust that his soul was right at the last with the Lord. He was a good soldier, one of the best.

I will never forget the time I asked Harry to give me a haircut. All he had were hand clippers. He set me down on an ammunition box and proceeded to cut. When I got up and looked in the little shaving mirror, I was horrified to see that my hair had been completely mutilated. He just stood back and laughed. Actually it really didn't matter, since I was able to cover it up with a helmet and get on with business.

That haircut was certainly better than the profes-
sional haircuts from a Vietnamese barber who worked
in our base camp. He would shave us with a straight
razor and use the electric clippers when we had power. Then one night he was shot outside the perimeter
while carrying an explosive charge, trying to blow up
our ammunition dump—he was a Vietcong in dis-
guise. I thought back to the many haircuts and shaves
he had given me, especially when he used that
straight razor over my throat.

While there were many close calls that year in
Vietnam, I experienced the protection of the Almighty
and came back in good shape from Southeast Asia.
Because of poor communications, certainly under-
standable under the difficult situation of battle, it was
once believed by some that I had become a casualty. It
happened around the time Chaplain Barragy was
killed in the helicopter. The chaplain of the engineer
battalion stationed near our base camp heard the report of the crash and the death of a chaplain over the
radio. He thought it was my name, Bowers, instead of
Barragy. So he sat down to write a letter to Doris con-
soling her. Before he mailed it, he thought better of it
and waited for confirmation of my "death." I've always been grateful that God spared Doris from receiving a false report.

The words General Paulick spoke to the basic
trainees at Fort Campbell came to mind:

> O Lord, lest I go my complacent way,
>   Help me remember out there somewhere
> A man died for me today.
>   So long as there be war,
> I must ask and answer,
>   Am I worth dying for?

During that year in Vietnam, there was not a

great deal of time to think about the reason we were there. We were busy trying to find and encounter the enemy and gain the upper hand. We realize now, looking back across the years, that it was a time of great heart-searching and confusion for most of us in the United States. Of course, from my point of view as a soldier in the army, I still find it difficult to understand the lack of patriotism and loyalty during those years.

It would be unfair to say that soldiers enjoyed the battle. They often went in the face of hostility at home. There were no brass bands with flags waving and crowds gathering to see them off. In fact, there was open defiance in many cases. It was a dirty, unpopular war. When I think about the men who went to Vietnam, I think of them as a special breed—going with cries of derision ringing in their ears from those who were well practiced in debate and dissent. They were going against the tide, it seemed. They knew that life was precious, but they also knew that freedom was priceless.

Two soldiers were once heard talking about their involvement in the military. One asked, "What made you go into the army?"

The other replied, "I had no wife and I loved war." Then he in turn asked, "What made you go?"

"I had a wife and I loved peace, so I went to preserve it for her."

Across the long years of the Vietnam War many servicemembers came and went in the Southeast Asian battle area. There was one common bond more widely observed than any other. It was the bond of patriotism, the love of country and of freedom that motivated them to offer their lives. Perhaps as we continue to look back across the increasing span of years to that period of our history, we will be able to see more clearly the real values of our freedom, our country, and all we hold dear.

The months soon grew into a year, and my time in Vietnam drew to a close. The days were filled with missions in various parts of South Vietnam. There were more dangerous missions in which God was very real to us. There was a constant schedule of services in a variety of places. I had learned to set up an altar with a few worship symbols in just about every condition imaginable. I found the task of chaplain to be a holy trust. The longer I served, the more rewarding it was to be a shepherd and guardian to our brave troopers on the forward edge of the battle area.

During the year we were there, we celebrated Christmas, of course. That's a little difficult for many Americans to do when the weather is around 110 or 120 degrees. Someone sent me a Santa Claus suit. I probably lost 10 pounds wearing it while going around to every orderly room and tent to play Santa Claus. One lieutenant sat on my knees and had his picture taken to send back home. He was killed a couple of months later.

At Christmas we invited some American missionaries to bring the Montagnards (mountain tribesmen) to sing to our men. It was a beautiful experience as, in their native costume, these Christians sang from Jer. 33:3: "Call unto me, and I will answer thee, and shew thee great and mighty things, which thou knowest not." One of the enduring memories of serving in Vietnam along with the sacrifices of the soldiers was the sacrifices these Christians faced as they held on to their faith in a country that was in great turmoil. As we now know, many of them literally gave their lives because of their belief in Jesus Christ. When the books are finally balanced, those warriors of the Cross who served as unsung heroes are going to find their side of the ledger well in the black. One of the things that comes out of most wars is an ongoing concern for the suffering and heartache left behind by the ravages of its battles. Hopefully the years will prove this to be true in Vietnam as well.

9

Home from the Field

The big day finally came, and I hitched rides with the air force over the mountains and down to the plains where the base camp was located. I grabbed my duffle bag and what little bit of belongings I had and went on down to Saigon. I hated to say good-bye to all the old-timers I had served with. There were also new men in the outfit now taking the places of those who were casualties. So it was time for those of us who had fought the first year in Vietnam to go home. This time the trip was by commercial plane instead of by slow boat.

I wrote to my parents to let them know I was on the way. Doris didn't know I was coming home, so when we got to San Francisco I called her. She quickly went to the hairdresser, got the kids all bundled up, and drove to Louisville, Ky., where I met them about midnight. One of the ironic twists of my homecoming was the fact that on the plane with me was Colonel Harlan Sanders, the Kentucky Fried Chicken tycoon. Since our youngest son, Steve, was only a year old when I left and had not really known me, he was more intrigued by the chicken colonel than by his own father. My father's heart understood his childish fascination. It was great to hold them all in my arms again.

Certainly my homecoming was much better than that of many veterans of Vietnam in the years that would follow. At least I was met with love and understanding, while many of them were spit upon and abused physically and emotionally when they stepped off the ship or plane that brought them back from the battle. Many of them had a more difficult battle to fight when they returned home than they had faced in Southeast Asia.

With the sights and sounds of the forward edge of a physical battleground behind, I now faced a battlefront of a different kind. I was assigned back to Fort Campbell as a division artillery chaplain. Here I served in a traditional chapel setting. One of the incidental battles to fight was the battle of the bulge as I began to gain weight. Of course, I had lost a great deal of weight in Vietnam—so it was back to getting in shape again and beginning to run with those special airborne troops.

Family life was especially enjoyable after having been away from my wife and growing children for an extended period of time. While I enjoyed the blessings of having my family with me, I began to see a ministry to those whose husbands and fathers were away. To meet this need, I began an organization called The Wives Who Wait. I found some real heroines among those great ladies, who faced the uncertainty of having husbands away at war. It was much more difficult to bring the death messages to the families at home than it was to bid farewell to the men who gave their lives on the battlefields. Here I saw the grief and the pain of dealing with the separation and loneliness in the faces of those who waited so faithfully.

A chaplain is sometimes looked upon as one who brings bad news as well as good news. This came home graphically when I made a trip into the mountains of Tennessee to find a sculptor to make a statue of an airborne soldier kneeling in prayer as a memorial to the fallen in Vietnam. This was to be set up outside our chapel. On the way there, I got lost and stopped at a farm home to ask directions. A young lady came to the door. As soon as she saw my uniform and the jeep outside, she ran screaming back into the house. In a few moments her mother came out very anxious and scared. She asked, "What do you want?" When she found out I was only asking directions, she cried, "Thank God! My daughter's husband is serving in Vietnam, and she thought you were the chaplain coming to tell her that he had been killed."

By this time in the war, many people were beginning to feel very hostile toward soldiers. At a graveside funeral service for a young soldier killed in Vietnam, I encountered feelings so hostile that when it was time to present the flag of a grateful nation to the widow, she responded, "I don't want that flag. My husband should never have been there."

She refused to take it. It was embarrassing, even though her anger was not directed against me personally. Her mother also refused to take it. The father refused it as well. Finally a grandmother took the American flag, possibly more out of courtesy to me than anything else. We had to deal with those feelings.

It wasn't long until the infantry battalion I was serving with was alerted for Vietnam. In fact, the entire division was alerted. I thought that meant having to go back. I struggled with the decision, which would mean being separated from the family again. It had been very difficult before on the children, who needed a role image of a father. When I found out the decision was mine, I determined that the forward edge of the battle this time was to stay at home to minister on this front with our family and the families who had to stay behind.

My life now became a series of encounters different from those experienced in Vietnam. One of the things it was possible to do while serving as a peacetime chaplain was to get involved in sports as a way to get close to the troops. God allowed me to develop some tennis skills and win some tournaments. I was honored to qualify for the all-army tennis team, where my partner, Bill Gardner, and I won two senior interservice tennis tournaments. This afforded several opportunities to "gossip the gospel." Once again we were finding ways to be close to the people I was sent to minister to by being more than just a man behind the pulpit or a counselor behind the desk.

There were other assignments: chaplaincy school; Fort Hamilton, N.Y.; and Fort Carson, Colo.

10

Guarding the Perimeter

At Fort Carson I was assigned to the Division Support Command. There I would often visit in the barracks a couple of hours before the service began and invite the soldiers to chapel. Quite frequently they would follow me on down to the worship service. Eventually Wrangler Chapel became a popular place for young single soldiers at Fort Carson.

To back this up, I would visit the personnel in the maintenance shops, hike with the troops to the field, and stay out there with them. The maintenance battalion commander, who became a major general, said years later that he appreciated this ministry of presence more than words could convey.

We started a literature crusade at Fort Carson. This really began in Japan when we started a chapel bookstore at Camp Zama. We saw our chapel community start to grow spiritually as they began to read Christian books.

At Carson came the chance to get a master's degree in alcohol rehabilitation at a major university. Because the ministry at Fort Carson seemed to have just begun, I chose to stay.

The time in Colorado was good for our family.

Our middle child, Bill, went through some times of adjustments and at a Christian youth camp gave his heart to Jesus. Our daughter, Sharon, chose to go to a Christian college to become a nurse; and our youngest son, Steve, was saved during those years. I shall always be grateful to our church family in Colorado Springs for their friendliness and outreach to us.

Of course, the mountains provided some great challenges to us all. It proved to be a good place to be during some of the growing-up years for our children. Skiing, backpacking, and mountain climbing built good memories.

In the midst of this productive time, orders came for me to go to Korea. For the first time in the military I honestly felt unable to cope with an assignment. I was going through a lot of personal struggle and perhaps a little bit of middle-age crisis. I had missed going to Korea as an enlisted man during the Korean War. We didn't look forward to another year of separation but knew it had to come sooner or later.

After a tearful good-bye, I flew to Seattle and heard the bad news in the airport that our tour had been extended one month longer. This was discouraging. Still I realized that God was near, and I was going again to a different battle area for another time of testing.

We arrived in Seoul in February. It was extremely damp and cold, which didn't help lift the spirits any. Nobody was at the plane to meet me, so and I hurried off with the rest of the soldiers on a bus to a replacement center. It was the weekend and there was not much action, so I settled in the room and called on some missionaries there. The Schuberts extended an invitation for an evening filled with fellowship.

An unexpected surprise was seeing Dr. Jerry

Johnson, who was there on official business as World Mission director for our denomination. But that night the room was so cold it was impossible to get warm. Feelings of loneliness crept in. This was a tour that could not really be made without God's great grace. To top it off, I became extremely sick with what I thought was kidney stones. I started to call the hospital and get an ambulance but toughed it out until the next morning. On the way to chapel the same pain hit again, and I finally had to go to the hospital that afternoon. They didn't find any kidney stones, and I was released.

Post chaplain for Camp Humphreys was to be my assignment. It proved to be one of the great ones. That shouldn't be a surprise, knowing that some of the greatest assignments are accompanied by severe testing. The first morning I was awakened early at four o'clock to majestic music. I thought maybe it was the Lord's second coming, and our family wouldn't have to go through this year of being separated. It turned out that the music was coming over the public-address system in the village to remind the Koreans that it was time for their early-morning prayer meeting.

Transportation was pretty tough to secure in Korea. At first I was dismayed but finally decided that if a military vehicle was not available, I would find another way. So I bought a bicycle at the post exchange. I would often ride it to the flight line and pedal up to the back of a Chinook helicopter and ask where they were going. I would then ride it up the ramp of the aircraft, tie it down, then sit in the jump seat with the men and gossip the gospel while flying all over Korea.

I felt like a military church planter, for here was

another opportunity to start a church in Camp Humphreys. There had not been much going on before we arrived. In addition to the traditional morning service, we started an evening service and prayer meeting. We would frequently get the hearing-impaired children to come from the orphanage nearby. Even though the men couldn't understand a word they sang, they would listen with tears in their eyes. The tunes to the hymns and songs were very familiar to us. The orphans were extremely poor, and frequently we would take up offerings and take things to them, especially at Christmas, Thanksgiving, and Easter.

One unforgettable Christmas I rode the bicycle out to the orphanage. It was below zero, and I put on all the clothes available to pedal out there. On the way back, I saw some kids ice-skating. They had only one pair of skates, and each skate was a different size. They would take turns, one skating while the others sat and watched. There was about two inches of snow on the ice, and I took the bicycle and rode out there with them. We didn't communicate much with words, but a lot with laughter.

We needed a spiritual awakening at Camp Humphreys, so I asked one of the missionaries from Seoul to be our speaker. There was a good nucleus of men who loved the Lord, and God gave us a real renewal. It was just before this meeting that our daughter back home got sick after climbing Pike's Peak. It was serious enough for them to take her to the hospital for emergency surgery. I was told, "It does not warrant an emergency leave, but it's up to you if you feel you can make it home." I loved our daughter and wanted to be close to her during her crisis.

I was torn between going home or staying in Korea and ministering to the troops as we prepared for God's visitation. I was the only chaplain there. Normally there were three chaplains assigned to Camp Humphreys, but the other two were on leave. I opted not to go home, but it was one of the hardest decisions in my life. God sent Christian friends to help Doris and to encourage Sharon. She pulled through fine.

We burned up the lines in phoning through the Military Affiliate Radio System (MARS) station, as my wife and daughter received frequent calls. It was terrible to be 6,000 miles from home, knowing one of our loved ones was in the hospital. Yet God was near.

During my time in the army, Al Freyez, a friend in our home church, prayed every day for me. I felt the power of prayer.

Because of choosing to minister not only to the chapel community but also to the three battalions assigned to the post, I spent a lot of time flying with the men of the Aviation Battalion. I became close to them and shared what they experienced in the long hours of flight all over Korea.

On one occasion the big Chinook I was flying on was carrying some American special forces and Korean airborne troops on a jump. I asked the pilot to call ahead and ask the commander if I could jump with them. He said to tell the chaplain to come to see him when the helicopter landed. He gave some instructions, and I started jumping with the Korean airborne and the special forces, again extending my ministry out beyond the people who were in my immediate installation. This helped in ministering to our American troops and some Koreans as well.

It was a delight to "hit the silk" again and to experience the exhilaration of being airborne. However, on one of the jumps I got caught in the high wind. I was being driven into the motor pool area, which was off the drop zone. I tried desperately to turn and get out of the way but was heading toward a quonset hut. It wouldn't have been that bad to crash through the roof of that hut and land on somebody's desk, but there were high-tension wires ahead. I cried out, "God, help me!"

I just missed those wires by 30 feet and landed on the side of the hill at probably about 25 miles per hour. I was a bit shaken up, but, thank God, He spared my life. Needless to say, it was a little more frightening to jump after that; but it was the better choice to get back at it lest I wouldn't want to jump anymore. It was best to keep that option open in case the Lord wanted me to go back with a unit like the 101st, so the jumps continued.

It was during my tour in Korea when Vietnam fell. It was a depressing time, and I identified with the low esteem and morale of the troops. It seemed to us that all the men we knew personally had died in vain. It was extremely difficult to bring hope and cheer during that dreary era. But nonetheless we kept on, and God blessed and honored our ministry.

In Korea I felt as close to God as I ever had. It seemed easier to serve Him without all the distractions such as television. Nevertheless, it was a hardship for Doris and the children.

They used to say that if the army wanted you to have a wife, they would have issued you one. Thankfully, that philosophy is passé now. The military services are now advocating programs that support strong family relationships.

The missionaries recognized the loneliness of our servicemembers and frequently invited us out for meals. We would help by bringing some American food to them so that we could enjoy it together.

We had a Korean maid who cleaned the chapel. She was a fine Christian woman who worked very hard. She had been through the Japanese occupation and the Korean War, and through it all she became a Christian. For Christmas that year the congregation bought her a coat to keep her warm during the bitter winter, but she didn't keep it long. She found someone else she thought needed it more. I wanted to get her something personal, so I bought her some hand lotion. She bubbled over with excitement and said, "Jesus knows, Jesus knows. Jesus knew I only had a little left in my bottle."

She never told anyone she needed any, but I got the exact kind she had always used to soften her hands from the scrub water and the coldness of the winters. Her face shone with the glory of God.

She found out my feet were always cold, so she knitted me some slippers. The chapel office was so cold that I would often take off my boots and wear the slippers to keep my feet warm. Before I left Korea, she took some of the gold that she had saved and had it hammered into a small cross for me to wear on my tie. I will never forget Mamasan. She was one of those special folks whose love for the Lord shone through all of her life. She worked at a menial job but did it well and for the glory of God.

Thank God for a wife who was conscientious and sensitive to the needs of the family, especially when I couldn't be there to serve in the capacity as spouse and father to my family. It didn't hinder their spiritual growth. God provided grace for Doris. She did all the things it normally takes two people to do, but she had extraordinary skill and wisdom.

It was a lonely time for both of us. I had never had a bird for a pet and never had any desire to have one, but it was so lonely when I went back to the trailer at night that I bought a canary and put him in a cage. At least I could hear some singing occasionally. It was probably at one and the same time the worst and the best year of my chaplaincy.

After one Sunday morning altar call, a battalion commander admitted, "Curt, you almost got me to come forward." I prayed all the more earnestly for him, as I still do, that he would become a Christian and give his heart to the Lord and know for sure that Jesus is Lord of his life.

The 13 months came to an end, and I left the Land of the Morning Calm, saying good-bye to the missionaries and to the congregation and heading for the airport. How great it was to get back in the Colorado mountains. Our family was together again. Little did we realize that I would be back in the Land of the Morning Calm almost 10 years later as Chaplaincy Ministries director, leading a servicemembers' retreat.

Soon it was down the mountain, across the plains and the central Texas region to a place called Fort Hood—the largest military installation in the free world. We arrived just at the time the bluebonnets were in full bloom and the March sun was beginning to warm the land. We welcomed a new church planting opportunity. Only a few families were attending our chapel, so it was a great challenge. Here I continued to fly with the men of the Sixth Air Cavalry Brigade.

God blessed in Blackhorse Chapel. We had three other chaplains—Art Skinner, Dick Bates, and Bill Gardner. We would get together weekly for prayer and worked well together as a team. We would eat with the troops in the mess hall. I would also stand in the line many times and serve food, inviting the troops to chapel, again reaching out in the ministry of presence.

I asked Chaplain Skinner to start a youth group. He did, and it became the best one on the entire post. Those young people still maintain their friendships and write to one another. Three attended colleges, and one graduated from seminary in 1988. Two are in full-time Christian service.

As a family we continued to enjoy the physical and spiritual growth of our children.

Again we started a chapel bookstore. As the men began to read about missions, they were challenged to support missionary work around the world. In fact, one of them, Capt. Bob Harrison, was called to leave the military to serve with Jungle Aviation and Radio Service. He married a lovely girl by the name of Becky. She didn't feel led to go to the mission field at first and wrestled with that decision for over a year. As it turned out, not only did God give Becky assurance, but she was almost more enthusiastic than Bob to go to New Guinea. She gave up 8 years of military service, and he gave up 12 years of service, to follow God's will.

It was their burden for missions and their exuberance and love that sparked the chapel congregation to want to give 25 percent of our offerings to missionaries. At first the staff chaplain said we couldn't give that much to missions because we needed to support the programs of our post. But we felt strongly that God was leading us to do it. The council finally agreed. God blessed the missionary vision, and we supported both areas of concern adequately. The interest in missions drew people to our fellowship, and the congregation increased numerically and in their giving as God blessed. Chaplain Van Vorce, the man who led me to Christ, preached a revival. Souls were saved and lives rededicated to serving the Lord.

After Korea I needed time with the family more than ever. The ministry here emphasized family relationships. We saw other families saved and filled with God's Spirit. Years after we left the chapel, it maintained a strong missionary outreach and had the reputation of being a "family" chapel.

Close to the end of my career I was assigned to Fort Knox, the place of my beginning in 1952. It was there I was privileged to speak to the graduates of basic training and look back with them across the years, remembering how God had guided my life. During these months and years came the realization that God had really given some unique experiences that I could now share with others who were soon to be going into their own battlefields.

At Fort Knox, family life took on tremendous meaning, and I had more time to share in the lives of our children. Thank God for the strength of our family. The constant moving demanded of military families can make them stronger emotionally and spiritually or bring about the disintegration of this basic unit of society. God really blessed us with a family that became strong and more closely knit as we traveled together.

Our last move took us to Fort Stewart, Ga., where I was assigned as the installation staff chaplain. It was February. In June our son Steve was set to finish high school, so I went down to my new assignment alone. This gave me another opportunity to realize the importance of ministering to men and women who are separated from their families. It wasn't long, however, before our family was back together, living on post.

Happy days were spent with Steve and Bill as we hunted deer and quail on different military posts.

In this assignment at Fort Stewart I continued the habit of trying to be with the troops wherever they were. Sometimes this meant eating with them in the mess hall or running with them early in the morning. Sometimes it meant having prayer with a young couple and their new baby, praising God for new life; or it sometimes involved an early-morning prayer meeting with the chaplains under my supervision. I thoroughly enjoyed serving under and ministering to two great generals: Maj. Gen. Jack Galvin and Maj. Gen. Norman Schwarzkopf, both of whom became four-star generals.

Chaplain Curt Bowers leading a service in observance of Martin Luther King, Jr., Day at Fort Stewart, Ga., with, *from left,* Maj. Gen. H. Norman Schwarzkopf of Fort Stewart; equal opportunity employment officers; the director of religious education at Fort Stewart; and Fort Stewart Deputy Staff Chaplain Jim Young.

11

Under New Orders

Some new orders came down for me in 1984, this time through the headquarters of my church rather than from the United States Army. I was asked to accept the position of Chaplaincy Ministries director in Kansas City. We prayed a long time before we left the ministry we loved. Finally feeling that God was asking us to bridge the gap between the chaplaincy, the servicemembers, and our church, we accepted our new orders.

At my retirement ceremony with all of its dignity, tradition, and ceremony, I had a very heavy heart. I was surrounded by my family, who had traveled long distances—our daughter, Sharon, who is an air force reserve nurse, now married to an F-16 pilot; Bill, our middle son, now a pastor; and Steve, working as a pharmaceutical salesperson and flying the Blackhawks in the National Guard. I was happy to become an endorser for our church but felt a deep sadness in leaving the special people God had called me to minister to. There was a closeness to the generals I served and the soldiers to whom I was privileged to minister. General Schwarzkopf shook my hand and hugged me as I stood in front of the military formation with tears in my eyes.

Now I am still traveling and supporting my denomination's chaplains and our uniformed personnel. The forward edge of the battle area has changed again for me in this new assignment.

What a privilege it is to serve on any forward edge in life! I thank God for the privilege of now representing my church and its service personnel (approximately 5,000 service people plus at least 7,500 spouses and children). It is my privilege to keep reminding the church of these sometimes unseen and often unsung heroes and heroines of our country who serve day and night as guardians of our frontiers.

While it was my privilege to serve on a very real battlefield at the front, many who read this book have battlefields and front lines of a different nature. Those of us who follow Christ are all called to immerse ourselves in the battle of life. None of us are called to stand on the sidelines or retreat to some quiet, secure place while life-and-death struggles are taking place all around us. We do not have that luxury as followers of Jesus Christ. So I pray for you. Whatever your assignment, take it gladly under the cross of Jesus Christ! May God find you faithful at the forward edge of your battle area.

From left, Maj. Gen. H. Norman Schwarzkopf
of Fort Stewart, Ga., and Chaplain Curt Bowers
in 1983, the year before Bowers' retirement
from the U.S. Army, cutting the cake at Fort Stewart
for the 208th anniversary celebration dinner
of the Army Chaplaincy Corps.